Saving the Earth to Save Humanity

Climate Revolution

I0131258

XU RUCHUAN

AMERICAN ACADEMIC PRESS

AMERICAN ACADEMIC PRESS

Published in the United States of America

By AMERICAN ACADEMIC PRESS

201 Main Street

Salt Lake City

UT 84111 USA

Email manu@AcademicPress.us

Visit us at http://www.AcademicPress.us

Copyright © 2024 by AMERICAN ACADEMIC PRESS

All rights reserved, including those of translation into foreign languages.

No part of this publication may be reproduced, stored in a retrieval system, or transmitted in any form or by any means, electronic, mechanical, photocopying, recording, or otherwise, now known or hereafter invented, without the prior written permission of the AMERICAN ACADEMIC PRESS, or as expressly permitted by law, or under terms agreed with the appropriate reprographics rights organization. Enquiries concerning reproduction outside the scope of the above should be sent to the Rights Department, American Academic Press, at the address above.

The scanning, uploading, and distribution of this book via the Internet or via any other means without the permission of the publisher is illegal and punishable by law. Please purchase only authorized editions and do not participate in or encourage electronic piracy of copyrighted materials. Your support of the publisher's right is appreciated.

ISBN: 979-8-3370-8912-6

Distributed to the trade by National Book Network Suite 200, 4501 Forbes Boulevard, Lanham, MD 20706

10 9 8 7 6 5 4 3 2 1

Manufactured in the United States of America

Contents

I. SAVING THE EARTH TO SAVE HUMANITY 1

II. CAUSES AND COUNTERMEASURES OF GLOBAL WARMING... 9

III. GLOBAL DESERTIFICATION CONTROL............. 20

(1) MULTIPLE FACTORS CONTRIBUTING TO GLOBAL WARMING 23

(2) ESTABLISHING NEW ECOSYSTEMS IN DESERTS...............24

(3) BENEFITS OF DESERT FORESTS 28

(4) NATURAL RESOURCES AND ENERGY AS MATERIAL BASIS FOR GLOBAL DESERTIFICATION CONTROL 31

(5) DEVELOPING WATER VAPOR IS KEY TO DESERTIFICATION CONTROL 33

(6) FRESHWATER IS A PREREQUISITE FOR DESERTIFICATION CONTROL 34

(7) THE INTERRELATIONSHIP BETWEEN THE THREE STRATEGIC MEASURES 35

(8) VARYING SITUATIONS REQUIRE DIFFERENT CONTROL METHODS..39

(9) TWO PERSPECTIVES WITH DIFFERENT OUTCOMES..........40

(10) GLOBAL ACTION UNDER THE UN FRAMEWORK 42

IV. DESERTIFICATION CONTROL OF THE SAHARA DESERT 46

(1) SHIFTING PERSPECTIVES, BUILDING CONFIDENCE 46

(2) PHASED IMPLEMENTATION 48

(3) AN IMMENSE CHALLENGE THAT ALSO CREATES WEALTH

OPPORTUNITIES..49

(4) URGENT NEED 51

(5) MOBILIZING CAPITAL 52

V. INCREASING GLOBAL FOREST COVER...............60

VI. CLIMATE REVOLUTION 67

(1) MAIN CAUSE OF GLOBAL WARMING..............................69

(2) THE HUMAN SURVIVAL CRISIS EXISTS 74

(3) TIME IS OF THE ESSENCE 77

(4) ESTABLISHING A NEW INTERNATIONAL ORDER 80

VII. THEORETICAL DISCUSSION ON CURBING GLOBAL WARMING 84

(1) EARTH'S HEAT BALANCE DETERMINES GLOBAL WARMING 86

(2) AN APPROPRIATE HEAT DISTRIBUTION RATIO IS REQUIRED 91

(3) MID-LATITUDE DESERTS AND MID-LATITUDE WESTERLY AIRFLOWS 95

(4) SOLAR ENERGY IS A DOUBLE-EDGED SWORD 101

(5) HIGH-ALTITUDE THERMAL ENVIRONMENT.................103

(6) CLIMATE CHANGE AND GLOBAL ECOLOGICAL ENVIRONMENT 105

(7) GENERATING WATER VAPOR IS A POWERFUL TOOL FOR CURBING GLOBAL WARMING 108

(8) SPREADING EFFECT OF ECOSYSTEM............................119

(9) COMPARISON OF TWO THEORIES.................................120

(10) THE THREE STRATEGIC MEASURES CAN CURB GLOBAL WARMING...125

I. Saving the Earth to Save Humanity

Deserts have expanded in size and number due to soil composition, climate change and human activities. The Sahara Desert, covered in grassland thousands of years ago, has now transformed into one of the driest places on Earth. The global desert area currently spans 31.4 million square kilometers, growing at an annual rate of 60,000km². Excluding the polar regions, deserts now constitute a quarter of the Earth's total land area. Apart from water, air and solar energy, a habitable Earth needs a balanced distribution of solar radiation between its surface and atmosphere. Disrupting this balance may result in dire consequences. When the atmosphere absorbs an excessive proportion of solar heat, it is detrimental to the ecological balance, eventually harming human health and destroying planet Earth.

At the beginning of its 4.6-billion-year history, the Earth was largely desert-free. The planet enjoyed an optimal distribution of solar energy during this period, with the surface absorbing more heat and the atmosphere absorbing less heat. These conditions fostered a favorable environment for the growth of living organisms, including the emergence of humans over a million years ago.

The gradual emergence and expansion of deserts have become a critical factor in changing the Earth's ecological conditions.

Global warming, a phenomenon that began with the emergence of deserts 10,000 years ago, is accelerating as desert areas expand.

The root cause of global warming is not carbon imbalance, but the thermal equilibrium of solar energy on Earth. Excessive heat in the atmosphere is the main issue. It determines the trend and direction of climate change, changes in global ecological conditions, and ultimately the survival of ecosystems.

Plants and animals cannot grow in deserts, and ecosystems will not exist in these areas to absorb and utilize solar radiation. This means that a significant portion of the heat absorbed by the desert surface is re-radiated into the atmosphere, thereby elevating atmospheric temperatures. Moreover, the desert size plays a crucial role in the distribution of solar energy between the Earth's surface and atmosphere. In other words, more heat is released into the atmosphere when deserts expand, exacerbating global warming. Thus, the Earth's energy imbalance is the leading cause of global warming. The global desert area stretches 31.4 million square kilometers. According to data from the Xinjiang Yearbook, solar radiation is 5,000-6,400 MJ/m2 per year in Xinjiang. Still, this data point is likely lower than the average for desert regions due to Xinjiang's higher latitude. It is estimated that global desert surfaces receive solar radiation equivalent to over 4 trillion tons of crude oil per year, of which more than 2 trillion tons are released into the atmosphere. In contrast, global carbon emissions from burning fossil fuels contribute about 4 billion tons of oil equivalent to the atmosphere each year — over 500 times lower than heat transferred from deserts. Are efforts in combating global warming heading in the wrong direction if we focus on the small proportion of heat (0.2%) contributed by carbon emissions, while disregarding the heat transferred to the atmosphere from deserts?

Mid-latitude deserts and mid-latitude westerly winds expand desert areas by 60,000 square kilometers each year, thereby adding the amount of heat equivalent to over 3.8 billion tons of crude oil to the atmosphere. However, the global energy conservation and emission reduction initiative can only reduce atmospheric heat by a maximum of 1 billion tons of oil equivalent per year, less than a quarter of the annual heat transfer increase caused by desert expansion. With rising heat released into the atmosphere, the energy conservation and emission reduction initiative alone cannot tackle global warming.

The interaction between mid-latitude deserts and westerly airflows is a terrifying force of destruction that will worsen desertification and increase the amount of solar heat transferred to the atmosphere, thereby intensifying global warming. Once the atmospheric heat exceeds the ecological redline, it will destroy the Earth's ecological conditions, gradually transforming a lively ecological Earth into a lifeless non-ecological planet. Natural disasters such as droughts, floods, typhoons, tsunamis, forest fires, mudflows and landslides will become increasingly severe and frequent. Humans will also face unprecedented calamities. Apart from deserts, non-desert areas with temperatures exceeding 54 degrees Celsius have already emerged. Ground temperatures of 55, 60, 65, 70 degrees Celsius will be recorded as atmospheric heat continues to increase and atmospheric temperatures rise. These conditions are also expected to last longer and become more extreme. How will people live in these environments? Some say: "We can stay indoors and turn on the air conditioner". But who will generate electricity for the air conditioner to run at 60 or 70 degrees Celsius? Who can survive when society comes to a standstill?

Average annual rainfall is the most significant factor affecting ecological conditions in areas with similar latitudes. A larger and hotter high-altitude thermal environment forms when atmospheric heat exceeds the Earth's ecological redlines. This is similar to high-altitude atmospheric thermal environments over deserts where there is limited condensation needed for rain, even with sufficient water vapor in the air. Desert areas only record a few millimeters of rainfall each year. Water vapor needs to flow to low-temperature ocean surfaces to condense and form rain. The increase in atmospheric heat changes the distribution ratio of rainfall between land and oceans, resulting in a significant decrease in rainfall on land and a rise in rainfall on ocean surfaces. Trees will dry up and die in large numbers when rainfall on land declines from an average of 800mm to 300mm, which will definitely happen if desertification is not reduced. Frequent forest fires will occur and more trees will be lost. There would also be no rain without trees, and no long-term water supply on land without perennial rivers, leading to the gradual disappearance of terrestrial organisms. Solar heat will increasingly be transferred to the atmosphere when land degradation occurs, raising temperatures and causing a large temperature variation between high-altitude areas and low-temperature ocean surfaces. A large amount of heat will be transferred to seawater, increasing seawater temperatures and harming the ecological conditions of marine organisms. When the Earth transforms from a an ecological planet full of life to an uninhabitable planet, it will become an ordinary member of the vast universe — a non-ecological planet. The black soil plains in the US will also struggle to produce food when land rainfall is below 300mm. Without food, millions of people will starve to death each year, and human extinction will become a consequence.

These are not sensationalized or groundless claims, but logical reasoning based on scientific data. The greatest danger lies in not being able to see the danger. Currently, deserts are not identified as the leading cause of global warming. It is a common misconception that carbon emissions are the largest contributor to climate change. The future and fate of Earth and humanity are at stake.

The root cause of global warming is the mutual interaction and effects of mid-latitude deserts and westerly winds, leading to the expansion of deserts and generation of excess atmospheric heat. This is a powerful force that can destroy the Earth. It is irreversible and if left unchecked, the Earth will eventually transform into a non-ecological planet.

The power of humans is insignificant compared to the power of nature. However, humans are intelligent. Leveraging the power of nature and human intelligence will develop a formidable force for change.

Excess atmospheric heat was initially the driving force behind the destruction of the ecological Earth and humanity. However, photosynthesis from afforestation, and the use of water and air can regulate, transfer and convert excess atmospheric heat into energy that forms ecosystems. This will eliminate the driving force of destruction and improve the Earth's ecological environment. Turning destruction into beauty is a result of human intelligence utilizing the power of nature. Only by reducing desertification can we save the Earth's ecosystems and humanity.

We must take urgent action and implement measures on global desertification control, increasing global forest cover, as well as energy conservation and emission reduction. These three inter-related approaches can control the accelerating trend of global warming to save the Earth's ecosystems and humanity.

Desert greening is the most effective desertification control measure. It can reduce the solar heat radiated from deserts to the atmosphere by more than half, transforming it into energy for new ecosystems and combating the excess atmospheric heat. It represents a green miracle where humans transform wasteland to forests. Desert greening is a successful experiment in planting trees on sandy soil, using the power of nature to tackle major problems that nature cannot solve.

Boundless deserts are daunting, and planting trees in deserts is unimaginable. Many doubt its feasibility as it feels like a distant goal that is impossible to reach.

Located at 38th parallel north, Saihanba National Forest Park in China's city of Chengde has built thousands of acres of forests, making it the world's largest man-made forest. The fact that the forests are growing in Saihanba is a strong indication that artificial forests can be built on sandy soil and create new ecosystems with water vapor flows. Saihanba currently has a forest cover of over 80%. For this reason, the United Nations Environment Programme awarded the Saihanba forest park as Champion of the Earth.

The Saihanba forest farm also experienced challenges in seedling cultivation as it is different to plant trees on sandy soil. Faced with the inability to cultivate seedlings using conventional methods, new techniques and processes were created to pave the way for afforestation on sandy soil, such as growing seedlings under lights and transplanting

7

seedlings.

The Saihanba forest farm is a beacon of hope amid the climate crisis. It bridges the gap between ideal and reality, and demonstrates that global desertification control is viable. It shatters the myth that planting trees in deserts is impossible, promoting confidence and determination in desertification control. Global desertification control also gives humanity the chance to survive in the future.

Te in China can control 40 acres of desert every day, plant 2000 trees per hour, and complete the workload of hundreds of people, greatly improving thehe three-dimensional sand fixing vehicle mad speed of sand control and realizing the dream of controlling global climate change as soon as possible.

II. Causes and Countermeasures of Global Warming

⚯

Global warming has drawn significant global attention as human survival is under threat. To tackle the climate crisis, the UN Climate Change Conference convened with the attendance of heads of state, and treaties such as the Paris Agreement were signed. These agreements required countries to conserve energy and cut emissions to control global warming.

This is a positive start to combat global warming, and serves as a platform for long-term cooperation among countries. It is also the first global cooperation of its kind, which is of great significance.

Is the increase in carbon dioxide concentration in the atmosphere the decisive factor in the rise of global temperatures? Can energy conservation and emission reduction stop global warming? Can human efforts alone curb and reverse climate change? Is it that easy to slow and reverse global warming? Is the power of humanity stronger than the power of nature?

Climate change and the ecological environment are

two aspects of human living. These two aspects are inter-related, affecting and constraining each other. There is sufficient water vapor and low temperatures over the oceans, while deserts experience a lack of water vapor and high temperatures, leading to changes in airflow and rise in temperatures.

Humans cannot directly control climate changes in high-altitude environments, but they can change the ecological conditions in ground environments. Changing the ecological conditions in ground environments can control corresponding changes in high-altitude locations, making this approach feasible and effective in curbing climate change.

Climate change is the norm as the Earth is undergoing climatic changes everywhere and at all times. Global warming is an abnormal state of climate change, a deterioration of the Earth's ecological environment. The land where humanity depends for survival is gradually vanishing due to desertification, while extreme weather and natural disasters will become increasingly severe and frequent. This is a warning of an impending survival crisis. The global community must take urgent action to mitigate global warming.

Rising temperatures and global warming require a source of heat. Thus, we must first address the question: What is the source of heat that causes global warming?

Carbon-based fuels are burned to produce carbon dioxide and generate heat for living spaces. However, carbon dioxide is not the source of heat that causes rising temperatures. The increase in carbon dioxide concentration in the atmosphere only increases the atmosphere's heat absorption capacity to a certain extent. Rising temperatures and greenhouse gases such as carbon dioxide can be regarded as "accomplices", while the source of excess heat is the real "culprit". Finding and reducing the source of increased atmospheric temperature is the key to addressing global warming.

The Earth's atmosphere heats up from the ground, and the amount of heat from the ground depends on the balance between solar radiation reaching the Earth and the Earth's surface heat. According to a diagram of Earth's heat balance, the surface absorbs 47% of the solar radiation reaching the Earth on average, 34% is radiated from the surface to the atmosphere, and the atmosphere absorbs 19% of the solar radiation. The amount of solar radiation directly absorbed by the atmosphere is relatively stable and can be considered a constant. Therefore, the total proportion of ground absorption and ratio of ground radiation transferred to the atmosphere can also be considered a constant at 81%. However, there was a significant variation in the ratios of ground absorption and ground radiation transferred to the atmosphere in different areas. In areas with a high forest cover, the solar radiation reaching the surface is primarily absorbed and utilized by the photosynthesis of trees and evaporation of water vapor from trees (heat of vaporization for water: 580 kcal/kg). The ratio of heat absorbed by the ground can be as high as 55%, and ground temperatures will not rise if there is less residual heat. In contrast, the proportion of ground radiation transferred to the atmosphere can drop to below 26%, maintaining atmospheric temperatures at normal levels. Heating of the ground occurs because there is no ecosystem to absorb solar heat since it is difficult for plants and animals to grow in deserts. Sandy soil, mainly composed of silicon dioxide, has a low specific heat capacity of only 0.23 cal/g-°C, which is less than a quarter of water's specific heat capacity. The same mass of sand and water absorbs the same amount of heat. The temperature of sand will rise by four degrees Celsius if the water temperature rises by one degree Celsius, resulting in the temperature increase of desert surfaces. Heat absorption is still relatively low even if the desert surface's temperature is high. This reduces the proportion of solar radiation absorbed by the desert surface to between 26% and 28%. However, the ratio of heat radiated to the atmosphere can be as high as 53%-55%. The ground temperature remains high even with lower proportion of heat absorption by the ground. This will heat the air near the ground before rising to create a high-altitude thermal environment and contribute to atmospheric temperature increase. As a result, the proportion of heat transferred from the desert surface to the atmosphere is more than double that of areas with high forest cover. The desert surface transfers most of the solar radiation to the atmosphere, becoming the main source of increased atmospheric temperatures.

Since solar radiation, the ground, and atmosphere are

in different locations in the same heat balance system, there is a quantitative relationship between the atmosphere's heat, which comes from the ground's solar radiation, and convective heat transfer of hot air rising from the ground. Hence, the meteorological conditions of temperature, pressure and humidity at a specific altitude in a particular area are determined by the ecological environment of the ground to a certain extent. In other words, improving the ecological environment of the ground is the basis for tackling climate change.

Climate change is driven by temperature differences. Temperatures at the higher range will have a greater impact on global warming. For example, it does not feel too hot at 32-34 degrees Celsius during summer, but 37-40 degrees Celsius will feel unbearably hot. Deserts are where high atmospheric temperatures are produced and the main source of heat for increased atmospheric temperatures, making them the largest contributor to global warming. Desertification control is the key to reducing high atmospheric temperatures and decreasing the heat transferred to the atmosphere, ultimately curbing global warming.

Deserts have the most severe ecological conditions on Earth, and they are the primary source of heat that cause rising temperatures. To address climate change, we must focus on global desertification control and afforestation in deserts.

Spanning 31.4 million square kilometers, deserts make

up a quarter of the Earth's total land surface — larger than the size of three China territories. With reference to the Xinjiang solar radiation energy data of 5,000-6,400MJ/m2 per year, the global desert surface receives solar radiation equivalent to 4 trillion tons of crude oil, transmitting over 2 trillion tons to the atmosphere each year. This is the largest source of heat that causes rising global temperatures. It is impossible to stop global warming by cutting carbon emissions alone and overlooking the importance of reducing desertification. Furthermore, it is more effective to use the power of nature to mitigate climate change, as relying on human efforts alone to conserve energy and cut emissions will not be enough.

Water vapor and carbon dioxide in the Earth's atmosphere do not produce heat per se, but affect the proportion of ground radiation absorption at 80% or 90%. However, absorbing 90% of 1,000 calories of heat is 10 times greater than absorbing 90% of 100 calories of heat. Thus, the heat transferred from the ground to the atmosphere provides the most crucial source of heat data.

Since the heat transferred from the desert surface to the atmosphere is more than double the heat transferred to the atmosphere from the ground in an area with high forest cover, the global desert surface receives 4 trillion tons of crude oil equivalent of heat each year. Assuming a 50% heat transfer rate to the atmosphere, this is equivalent to 2 trillion tons of crude oil, or 200 times the amount of carbon energy consumed globally each year. With such a large amount of heat released to the atmosphere, how can temperatures not rise? Can we overlook such a major cause? Judging from the figures alone, solar heat from large deserts is the main source of heat causing rising global temperatures and global warming.

To reduce the heat transferred from the desert surface to the atmosphere, trees must be planted in deserts to increase forest cover. In addition, afforestation will allow trees to absorb most of the heat transmitted to the ground, lowering ground temperatures, reducing the heat transferred from the ground to the atmosphere, and curbing global warming. Hence, afforestation in deserts has significant potential to reduce heat transfer from the ground to the atmosphere.

At a high temperature of 40 degrees Celsius, the ground temperature is 3-5 degrees Celsius lower in a forest. In contrast, ground temperatures can reach 60-65 degrees Celsius in deserts, which is usually 20-30 degrees Celsius higher than ground temperatures in forests. According to the radiation heat transfer theory, the intensity of heat radiation emitted by matter is proportional to the fourth power of the matter's absolute temperature. Afforestation in deserts can lower ground temperatures by 20-30 degrees Celsius, significantly reducing the heat transmitted from the ground to the atmosphere. Afforestation has four main functions in deserts: 1. Lowering ground temperatures and significantly reducing the amount of ground radiation transferred to the atmosphere, directly combating climate warming. 2. Reducing the amount of hot air rising from the ground, preventing the formation of a hot environment at high altitudes and lowering atmospheric temperatures. 3. Increasing forest cover, water vapor and rainfall, as well as improving ecological conditions. 4. Forests act as converters in forests, transforming resources and energy, such as desert surface, solar energy, and water, into forest products for economic and ecological benefits that are 10 times greater. These four functions are crucial in mitigating global warming.

Other measures can also be implemented. For example, building solar power plants in deserts can generate solar energy and reduce the heat transferred to the atmosphere. Developing solar energy is an excellent solution for energy issues. However, it cannot improve ecological conditions and create a livable environment. On the other hand, the desert area that can be used to build power plants is negligible compared to the total desert area. Thus, solar power plants are unlikely the main means of addressing global warming. However, they can be combined with afforestation to tackle climate change. Desertification control requires a forest cover rate exceeding 60%, leaving less than 40% of unforested land for various public facilities and residences. Building rooftops can also be equipped with solar panels to generate power and increase solar energy utilization, further reducing heat transfer to the atmosphere. This approach also improves land use efficiency.

Another major cause of global warming is the significant decline in global forest cover.

The Earth's forest area was 5.5 billion hectares in 1862, but decreased by more than half to 2.6 billion hectares in the 1970s. This led to a dramatic rise in the amount of heat transmitted from the ground to the atmosphere and a considerable decrease in forest carbon sequestration and oxygen release capacity. Extensive deforestation is a slow form of suicide for humanity. Timber harvesting should be regulated, where logging is limited within a specific area to maintain forest cover and timber reserves. Artificial forests can also be developed to increase forest cover.

The UN Climate Change Conference should prioritize forest cover increase, specifying targets and timelines for increasing forest cover based on the circumstances of each country. Global desertification control, increasing forest cover, as well as energy conservation and emission reduction are associated with one another, and combining these three measures will achieve the goal of stopping global warming. Global warming is an issue that determines the future and fate of humanity and future generations. The three recommended measures prioritize human involvement and utilizes the power of nature to address global warming. Every country, individual, piece of land, and tree in the world can be mobilized as a powerful force to tackle global warming. As long as humans are adept at utilizing the power of nature, they can amplify their own power to curb global warming and overcome the survival crisis. Utilizing the power of nature is the fundamental solution to climate change.

Global ecological conditions and climate change are two aspects of humans' living environment. The three strategic measures can optimize our living environments, controlling the channels of temperature rise from natural and man-made causes to combat global warming.

The strategic measures require action from all individuals, and conducted under the United Nations framework to promote global cooperation.

The UN Climate Change Conference must boost its influence and lead global efforts to address climate change, formulating legally-binding agreements for countries to implement, such as the Convention to Combat Desertification and Convention to Increase Global Forest Cover.

The UN Climate Change Conference should also convene on a regular basis, and establish a permanent body to devise long-term strategic and action plans on global warming. This institution can set tasks and requirements, with the power to urge countries to take action in jointly combating global warming. A United Nations Desertification Control Committee should also be established to lead global efforts in reducing desertification.

China is a major power that will not seek hegemony. However, China can unite the world to take concrete actions in tackling climate change, such as diverting water to Xinjiang for desertification control. China can become a climate leader with its vision, determination, responsibility and commitment in global desertification control. Under the United Nations framework and the goal of a "shared future for mankind", we must work together to save humanity. China can then earn the respect and trust of people worldwide, and make greater contributions to the world.

III. Global Desertification Control

Global warming will increase the frequency and intensity of natural disasters and extreme weather, such as El Nino, droughts, floods, typhoons, hurricanes, high temperatures, cold waves, and sandstorms, causing desertification and destruction on land that humans depend for survival. The interaction and effect of mid-latitude deserts and mid-latitude westerly winds have already claimed half of the land in mid-latitude areas, expanding at the current rate of $60,000km^2$ per year. In 150 years, a new Sahara Desert will be formed, and two more Sahara Deserts will be formed in another 300 years. Humans will be forced to live in Siberia and Alaska, shrinking the size of livable environments. In the battle for survival, endless wars will erupt, millions of families will be torn apart, displaced persons will surge, while diseases and hunger will create countless tragedies. Global warming will melt glaciers, raise sea levels, and viruses and bacteria from thousands of years ago will strike. Humanity will also face new infectious diseases that are more contagious and deadly. The COVID-19 pandemic has already threatened public health. How can we fight against more viruses?

Unprecedented climate disasters are likely to occur,

with temperatures of 55, 60, 65, and 70 degrees Celsius. Rainfall will decrease significantly and food cannot be produced, causing millions of people to starve each year. This will be a time when Earth descends into hell.

Cold waves have been sweeping across the globe in recent years, with snow falling in Fujian and Guangdong — provinces that do not usually experience snowfall. The heavy snow of six years ago returned this year. Some question whether the climate is warming or cooling. Some areas had never experienced snow, but are now snowing after global warming. Why is this happening?

Global warming is a long-term increase in the Earth's atmospheric temperature that cause abnormal weather patterns. However, snowfall in Fujian and Guangdong is a localized, short-term decrease in temperature — a climate change anomaly. Are these two events related? What is the relationship between them?

Global warming causes the melting of glaciers, absorbing a significant amount of heat (heat of fusion of ice: 80kcal/kg), generating a large amount of cold air, and forming southward cold waves during winter — a natural phenomenon that occurs every year. However, the intensity and travel distance of cold waves are related to the severity of global warming. A cold wave swept across 5,000-6,000 kilometers with tremendous force during the snowfall in Guangdong and Fujian. Where does this force come from?

Temperature variation is the driving force of airflow. More glaciers will melt in the Arctic as global warming intensifies, absorbing more heat and producing cold air with lower temperatures, while the Southern hemisphere has higher temperatures — creating a large temperature variation. This large temperature difference increases the driving force that forms cold waves, causing snowfall in Fujian and Guangdong. It might have snowed in Fujian and Guangdong, but the underlying cause or driving force is intensified global warming. It is a sign that global warming is getting worse.

Heat waves and droughts during summer and extreme cold waves during winter are manifestations of accelerating global warming.

Solely relying human efforts in energy conservation and emission reduction has not been able to curb global warming over the years. Instead, the effects of global warming have worsened. We must stop our illusions and depend on the power of nature. The three strategic measures of global desertification control, increasing global forest cover, as well as energy conservation and emission reduction must be implemented simultaneously to tackle global warming.

With an annual increase of $60,000km^2$ of desert area worldwide, global warming is speeding towards catastrophe, and humanity will experience a survival crisis. There are currently no proven solutions, but humanity cannot sit idly by and wait for death. We must find a way out.

(1) Multiple factors contributing to global warming

Climate change will present humanity with a dire survival crisis. Apart from the increased concentration of carbon dioxide in the atmosphere, there are other more significant factors that contribute to global warming. The main causal factor is large desert areas transferring most of the heat from solar radiation to the atmosphere, leading to excess heat and decrease in forest cover.

Deserts are the main source of heat for the rise in atmospheric temperatures as they re-transmit most of the solar heat to the atmosphere. Thus, reducing desertification is vital in combating global warming.

Vast desert regions need more freshwater resources and trees to increase forest cover, and utilize the photosynthesis and transpiration of trees to absorb and use solar heat. With less residual heat, ground temperatures will drop, reducing the heat transferred from the ground to the atmosphere and reversing global warming.

Global forest cover can increase from the current 22% to 40% if forest cover exceeds 60% in deserts worldwide, and there is tree cover gain in other areas. This will significantly reduce the amount of heat transferred from the Earth's surface to the atmosphere, and slow down global warming. Moreover, forest gain will improve the Earth's ecological environment. Desert greening not only reduces the amount of heat transferred to the atmosphere, but also hot air rising from the ground, thereby lowering atmospheric temperatures. It also sequesters carbon and releases oxygen to decrease carbon dioxide concentration in the atmosphere, increase negative oxygen ions, and improve air quality. To effectively control global warming, the three measures of global desertification control, increasing forest cover, as well as energy conservation and emission reduction must be implemented simultaneously to complement one another. However, global desertification control is the most challenging task and will be further discussed.

(2) Establishing new ecosystems in deserts

An ecosystem consists of biological communities and their living environments. Natural ecosystems cannot survive in deserts due to their harsh ecological conditions, preventing solar energy from being absorbed and utilized by ecosystems and leading to a substantial increase in the amount of heat transmitted from the ground to the atmosphere. Hence, it is essential to use freshwater resources to plant trees in deserts, establish new ecosystems with water vapor to absorb heat, and reduce the amount of heat transferred from the ground to the atmosphere.

Tree root systems are strong and extend deep into the soil, tolerating different soil conditions to give trees vitality and making it possible to establish new ecosystems in deserts.

Can new ecosystems be created in deserts?

The Saihanba forest farm in China has built thousands

of acres of forests, making it the world's largest man-made forest. It represents a green miracle of transforming wasteland into forests and is a successful experiment in planting trees on sandy soil. The fact that the forests are growing and surviving in Saihanba over the past 60 years is a strong indication that artificial forests can be built on sandy soil and create new ecosystems with water vapor flows. The park currently has a forest cover of over 80%. For this reason, the United Nations Environment Programme awarded the Saihanba forest farm as Champion of the Earth.

The Saihanba forest farm also experienced challenges in seedling cultivation as it is different to plant trees on sandy soil. Faced with the inability to cultivate seedlings using conventional methods, new techniques and processes were created to pave the way for afforestation on sandy soil, such as growing seedlings under lights and transplanting seedlings.

In China's Gobi Desert, pits were dug and soil was transported from dozens of kilometers away to fill the pits for planting trees. Through decades of tree-planting, the Gobi Desert has turned into a green desert and was designated as a national garden city, with a green cover of 39.23% and $36m^2$ of green space per capita. It is evident that humans can reduce desertification by utilizing natural resources and energy. Global desertification control is achievable, as long as we are determined in taking action.

Agricultural cultivation and afforestation are different.

Crop cultivation is done every year, including tilling, sowing, watering, and harvesting. This process is repeated and requires a large workforce. On the other hand, afforestation does not involve a lot of labor, with its impact accumulating over time. For example, 5.4 million square kilometers of trees would need to be planted in the 9 million square kilometer-Sahara Desert to reach a 60% forest cover. If this is completed over 100 years, 54,000km^2 of tree-planting would be needed every year. Each participating country only needs to complete a few thousand square kilometers of afforestation every year. China cultivates over a million square kilometers of farmland each year, and only a few thousandths of this area can be used for afforestation, making it a feasible strategy. Reducing desertification in the Sahara Desert is also achievable through global cooperation.

There is ample evidence that global desertification control is effective.

Freshwater resources can be used in deserts to conduct large-scale afforestation and replenish the water required for young trees. Once a large number of seedlings survive for five years, ground temperatures will gradually decrease, hot air will no longer rise, and heat will not exist at high altitudes. These conditions will further enhance condensation and increase rainfall. After 10 years, young trees will grow into forests, and large-scale forests will generate water vapor that can condense for increased rainfall. When total rainfall increases to sustain the growth of forests after 15 years, the use of external water sources can be gradually reduced. This allows water resources to be used for afforestation in other deserts, with a single water source repeatedly utilized in multiple locations. New ecosystems can also be created and expanded. This is known as the spreading effect of ecosystems, making it possible to control desertification on a large scale. Hence, this spreading effect plays a crucial role in greening deserts worldwide.

However, the vastness of deserts makes afforestation challenging. The Sahara Desert alone is as large as the United States, and the amount of water that can be diverted is inadequate for tree growth. Once forests have grown, they rely on an increasing amount of water vapor condensation and rainfall to eliminate the thermal environment. Rainfall is required for the growth of new forests in deserts.

Based on the available water volume, artificial forests can be developed in specific areas of deserts. The area of new man-made forests will gradually expand through the spreading effect, developing in phases. While this may take longer, the goal of greening global deserts can still be achieved. Without the spreading effect, global afforestation in deserts would be impossible.

Land, which occupies a quarter of the Earth's surface, receive sunlight equivalent to 4 trillion tons of crude oil each year and billions of cubic meters of freshwater are available every year. These unused resources can be transformed into forest products that increase ecological wealth, and improve ecological conditions through afforestation. Afforestation in deserts can convert wasted resources and energy into wealth. These resources and energy form the material basis for global desertification control. Coupled with the spreading effect of the ecosystem, nature's three major resources and energy enable afforestation activities to continue, promoting confidence in global desertification control. Global desertification control can then be achieved through the unwavering efforts of future generations.

Global desert greening is a challenging task for humanity — a long journey that will take hundreds of years, or even longer. In the 10,000-year history of mankind, a century or two is short. If humans can overcome the survival crisis and build a beautiful home on Earth, this will be a significant contribution to humanity's salvation and rewrite human history.

(3) Benefits of desert forests

Deserts are vast and can accommodate external freshwater resources, making them ideal locations for developing man-made forests. There are four major benefits building artificial forests in deserts.

1. Curbing desertification in mid-latitude regions

The interaction between mid-latitude westerly winds and mid-latitude deserts creates a vicious cycle that accelerates desertification in mid-latitude regions. Occupying half of the land in mid-latitude regions, deserts continue to expand. Desertification must be reversed in mid-latitude regions as it worsens the Earth's ecological environment and poses a threat to human survival.

While we cannot directly control westerly winds at high altitudes, we can reduce desertification to control airflows in a westerly high-altitude current. First, we need to plant trees in deserts, and gradually weaken the relationship between deserts and westerly winds, where they complement each other. High-temperature air will not rise from the ground when a desert is transformed into an oasis, eliminating a transmission point for high-altitude westerly winds. Multiple deserts transformed into oases will eliminate more transmission points for high-altitude westerly winds, weakening the airflows that wreak havoc. Furthermore, transforming deserts into oases will create green corridors in mid-latitude regions, adding multiple "lungs" to our planet for enhanced livability and combat global warming.

2. Reducing land surface and atmospheric temperatures

Forests evaporate a large amount of water vapor, which requires significant heat absorption. Photosynthesis converts solar heat, water, and carbon dioxide into chlorophyll, driving the energy flow and material circulation of the ecosystem and promoting the growth of trees. The two functions of evaporation and photosynthesis lead to increased utilization of solar heat for ecological purposes, creating less residual heat, lowering ground temperatures, and reducing the amount of heat transfer to the atmosphere to curb global warming.

3. Stabilizing climate change

Large-scale forests in deserts will increase local rainfall, alleviate droughts, lower ground and air temperatures, and reduce diurnal, topographical and geographical temperature variations. This will weaken the driving force of climate change, reduce sandstorms and hurricanes, as well as mitigate the impact of natural disasters. Forests in deserts will become climate change stabilizers.

4. Controlling carbon dioxide

Carbon dioxide, solar energy and water can be converted into chlorophyll through photosynthesis, absorbing and solidifying carbon dioxide from the air. Each hectare of broad-leaved forests can absorb one ton of carbon dioxide and release 727kg of oxygen daily. Global desert greening will significantly reduce the concentration of carbon dioxide in the atmosphere.

Carbon dioxide is a double-edged sword. It is not always the case that it is better to have less carbon dioxide in the atmosphere. While excess carbon dioxide can cause global warming that threatens human survival, insufficient carbon dioxide would lead to a shortage of raw materials for photosynthesis, resulting in less food production and hunger.

Global forest cover is still low, and photosynthesis of

plants is unable to control the rising carbon dioxide concentration in the atmosphere. However, the total amount of carbon dioxide that global forests can absorb will exceed the total amount of carbon dioxide produced each year when global forest cover increases twofold. Thus, forests in deserts can regulate the total amount of carbon dioxide in the atmosphere.

When there is high carbon dioxide concentration in the atmosphere, photosynthesis will intensify and a large amount of carbon dioxide will be solidified to produce food crops. On the other hand, photosynthesis will weaken when there is low carbon dioxide content in the atmosphere. Forests can regulate and maintain the carbon dioxide content in the atmosphere at a suitable level, allowing plants to grow, provide food for humans, and ensure human survival. Regardless of whether forests are a climate change stabilizer or a carbon dioxide concentration regulator, it will improve the global ecological environment.

(4) Natural resources and energy as material basis for global desertification control

The remarkable effects of desert greening stem from the unprecedented scale at which it utilizes natural resources and energy. Natural resources and energy can be turned into wealth.

1. Water resource utilization

Trillions of cubic meters of freshwater that would

31

otherwise flow into the sea can be used to plant trees in deserts. Desert land and solar energy can also be turned into effective resources that form a strong material basis.

2. Land utilization

Excluding the polar regions, deserts constitute a quarter, or 31.4 million square kilometers of the Earth's land surface. Deserts are the root cause of extreme weather conditions and natural disasters. They can be transformed into oases after reducing desertification, becoming effective land resources, increasing the Earth's effective land resources by one-third, enhancing forest cover, and improving the ecological environment.

3. Solar energy utilization

With reference to Xinjiang's solar radiation energy data of 5,000-6,400MJ/m2 per year, planting trees in over two-thirds of the world's deserts will see forest cover exceeding 60%, and solar energy utilization reaching 45% in afforestation areas. In addition, 1.2 trillion tons of crude oil equivalent of solar energy will be used for evaporation and the growth of artificial forests. Artificial forests also absorb and solidify large amounts of carbon dioxide, reducing the carbon dioxide concentration in the atmosphere. Man-made forests produce a large amount of water vapor, increasing rainfall and improving ecological conditions. The global energy consumption from fossil fuels, including oil, coal and natural gas, stood at 9.2 billion tons of crude oil equivalent. In other words, trees made up two-thirds of the world's deserts, and solar energy that can be used in a year is 120 times greater than the global energy consumption from fossil fuels. This huge amount of energy cannot be supplied or compared to human capabilities.

The utilization of these three wasted resources on Earth forms the material basis in addressing climate warming, improving the Earth's ecological environment, and building livable environments.

(5) Developing water vapor is key to desertification control

Water vapor serves as the raw material for rainfall. Thus, rainfall can only occur when there is enough water vapor content in the atmosphere. The two main sources of water vapor on land are water vapor transported over the ocean during monsoons, and water vapor generated from forests and surface evaporation. Inland areas with high forest cover experience more rainfall. Located 600km from the coast, Jiangxi province's Yichun has 60% forest cover and an average annual rainfall of 1,600-1,700mm. In contrast, the average annual rainfall of Hangzhou is lower at 1,100-1,500m, despite being located near the coast at a similar latitude. This is because Yichun generates more water vapor, while Hangzhou has less water vapor transported over the ocean. This suggests that water vapor generated from forests can rival water vapor transported over the ocean as a source of rainfall. In areas that lack water vapor transported over oceans, afforestation can generate more water vapor to increase rainfall. The average annual rainfall will reach at least 600mm if forest cover is 60% or higher in forested areas. Even if there is a lack of water vapor transported over the ocean, rainfall from the condensation of water vapor in forests can still maintain ecological conditions.

Increasing forest cover to a specific level is necessary for improving ecological conditions and increasing rainfall for the growth of trees.

The "spreading effect of ecosystems" can only function when forest areas are of a certain size and forest cover reaches specific levels. The effect will not be apparent if forest cover is below this threshold. The generation of water vapor from forests promotes the "spreading effect of ecosystems" and desertification control.

(6) Freshwater is a prerequisite for desertification control

The supply of freshwater resources determines the success of desertification control and afforestation. Rainfall is the main source of freshwater on land. However, rainfall utilization is low, as it flows into the sea through rivers. About 40-45 trillion cubic meters of freshwater flows into the sea through rivers. The minimum amount of freshwater needed for afforestation in deserts and arid areas is less than 5% of the freshwater flowing into the sea, or less than 200 million cubic meters each year. Based on specific conditions, methods such as water diversion, rainwater harvesting, water catchment, and water pumping can provide the freshwater needed for afforestation. For example, the Sahara Desert can source water from the Congo River through diversion and pumping. China's deserts can source water from Tibet, while the Arabian Desert can source water from the Congo River through diversion or pumping. Australia can build diversion canals, collecting water that would otherwise flow directly into the sea. Freshwater supply issues can be solved as long as we have the determination to reduce desertification and droughts.

(7) The interrelationship between the three strategic measures

The fundamental differences between solely focusing on energy conservation and emission reduction and the three strategic measures are discussed below.

Focusing solely on energy conservation and emission reduction assumes that atmospheric heat cannot be changed and the only solution to global warming is cutting carbon emissions. The three strategic measures are based on the principle that humans can harness the power of nature to reduce atmospheric heat.

Both natural and human factors contribute to global warming. Global desertification control and increasing forest cover can mitigate the impact of natural causes, while energy conservation and emission reduction can reduce the effects of man-made causes. These three strategies are essential in tackling climate change.

Global desertification control and increasing forest cover are improvements over energy conservation and emission reduction.

Energy conservation and emission reduction involves the cutting of carbon emissions, making use of human efforts to reduce rising man-made greenhouse gas emissions and minimize the human impact on climate change. However, the power of nature is stronger than the power of humans, and the impact of human activities on global warming is limited compared to the influence of natural factors.

Global desertification control and increasing forest cover utilize the powerful forces of nature to enhance the Earth's water cycle, carbon cycle and oxygen cycle. These two measures have multiple functions to improve the Earth's heat balance.

On the other hand, energy conservation and emission reduction has a limited effect on global warming.

Global desertification control and increasing forest cover significantly reduce the heat transferred to the atmosphere, regulating the sources of heat that contribute to global warming. With a global forest cover of 40%, trees have a large-scale impact as it can sequester carbon and release oxygen. Furthermore, carbon sequestration will continue to strengthen as trees grow.

Energy conservation and emission reduction is the

preliminary stage in fighting against global warming.

Meanwhile, desert greening and increasing forest cover are the crucial stages in tackling climate change.

Most of the solar heat transmitted from the desert surface to the atmosphere is the main source of global warming. Thus, global desertification control is the foundation of the three strategic measures, while increasing forest cover consolidates and complements the effectiveness of global desertification control. New deserts and wasteland will emerge if forest cover decreases and exposed surfaces increase, accelerating desertification and weakening the effectiveness of global desertification control. Therefore, increasing forest cover is vital in consolidating the effectiveness of desertification control. Furthermore, increasing forest cover reduces the heat transferred from the Earth's surface to the atmosphere, accelerates the process of reversing global warming, and improves the Earth's ecological environment to achieve the goal of building livable environments. Hence, increasing forest cover is necessary for reducing desertification.

The power of nature is immense, while the power of humans is minuscule by comparison. The key to addressing global warming is humans using their intelligence to harness the power of nature. The combination of human intelligence and the power of nature will be a formidable force in changing the world.

The world currently consumes nearly 10 billion tons of crude oil equivalent of carbon-based energy in a year.

Even with vigorous energy conservation and emission reduction efforts, we can only reduce the heat transferred to the atmosphere by less than 4 billion tons of crude oil equivalent. In contrast, the global desert surface transfers heat equivalent to 2 trillion tons of crude oil to the atmosphere — 500 times greater. This means that energy conservation and emission reduction only account for 0.2% of the amount of heat released to the atmosphere. If the sum of these two parts of heat transfer to the atmosphere is 100%, it is impractical to focus on the 0.2% of heat transferred to the atmosphere through energy conservation and emission reduction while neglecting the 99.8% of heat transmitted from global deserts. It is also impossible to achieve the goal of curbing global warming.

The global desert area currently expands 60,000km^2 every year, and global warming is worsening. Focusing on energy conservation and emission reduction to address climate warming and not prioritizing global desertification control, or focusing only on 0.2% and neglecting the 99.8%, can be described with the Chinese saying of "picking up a sesame seed only to lose a watermelon". Focusing on human-driven energy conservation and emission reduction alone leads to humans overlooking other effective countermeasures, delaying and wasting precious time amid the looming survival crisis. The negative effects of this approach outweigh the positive effects, and time determines our fate and future.

Misleading information is harmful, making us lose sight of progress. There is a need to address misconceptions to steer us in the right direction to fight against climate change. It is also vital to implement the three strategic measures to tackle global warming.

(8) Varying situations require different control methods

Deserts are predominantly located in mid-latitude regions. However, their distribution, geographic location and proximity to water resources vary, requiring different approaches to desertification control based on their conditions.

1. Some deserts are located in poor countries, posing a challenge to desertification control, such as the Sahara Desert. The UN Climate Change Conference needs to coordinate and mobilize countries to jointly control these deserts.

2. The UN Climate Change Conference should formulate a unified plan for deserts in economies with strong growth, such as Australia, China, India, and the United States, setting standards and timelines for these countries to implement desertification control measures. These countries should self-finance desert greening.

3. There are also deserts in countries with the financial means but lack water resources to reduce desertification, such as the Arabian Desert. The UN Climate Change Conference should take the lead in coordinating the diversion of water from the Congo River to the Arab region,

exchanging oil for freshwater and adopting afforestation and desertification control.

The Sahara Desert makes up a third of the world's total desert area, while the remaining two-thirds are scattered across multiple countries. If we can control the deserts scattered across various countries, we would have fulfilled a major part of the task to combat desertification and global warming.

Establishing an international cooperation platform is needed to reduce desertification in the Sahara Desert. However, the second and third situations described above can be implemented now.

Global warming threatens the survival of humanity. The UN should establish a global bank for desertification control to support countries in combating desertification and also assist with the desertification control of the Sahara Desert. Medium- and high-income countries should contribute funds to promote the message that global desertification control can ensure the survival of humanity. Financiers and entrepreneurs concerned about the future of future generations should also be welcomed to invest in the bank. Only then will successors have the opportunity to inherit and manage a lasting legacy, which can appreciate in value to increase personal and social wealth. This is a wise choice beneficial to humanity and future generations.

(9) Two perspectives with different outcomes

Are deserts a burden, nuisance, and liability? Yes and

no. Deserts will become a burden, nuisance, liability, and destructor of the environment if we treat it with indifference. On the contrary, there is potential for economic development if deserts are well-managed.

Desertification control can transform wasted land, water, and solar energy into raw materials for natural, low-cost production — turning them into wealth. They can become a foundation for improving the ecological environment, curbing global warming, and contributing to human survival. Hence, there are two perspectives on deserts with two different outcomes.

Deserts are the "tumors and wounds" on Earth, acting as heat transfer stations for global warming. Global desertification control eliminates the root cause of climate change, restoring vitality and determining the future of our environment.

We should view global desertification control from the perspective of tackling climate change and saving humanity. We need to be forward-looking, confident, overcome obstacles, and adopt afforestation in deserts. This will change the world, reshape landscapes, build a beautiful home on Earth, and address global warming.

We cannot combat global warming and improve the ecological environment without desertification control.

Deserts are extremely bad for the environment, with the most severe ecological conditions. Desertification is the worst-case scenario in the fight against global warming.

Thus, afforestation in deserts is a desperate countermeasure for climate change. Afforestation can only succeed in deserts. It can improve, and not destroy the environment. There are only returns and no risks as it is an investment backed by natural resources, and a contribution to humanity.

The expansion of deserts will destroy humanity. Can we stand idly by and let humans go extinct?

(10) Global action under the UN framework

Environmental degradation serves as a warning that the world is a global village, and each country is merely a household in this village. No country can stand alone and be detached from the world. The ecological conditions of countries cannot be improved if the global ecological environment deteriorates. Contributing to desertification control creates the conditions for improving the ecological environment of our countries.

Tackling global warming is a requirement for humanity to secure its survival. The UN has the responsibility to ensure all countries play a role in climate action.

In the past, the United Nations' main responsibility was to maintain world peace. Changing with the times, it is now necessary to protect our planet and curb global warming. Another way to maintain peace is guiding countries to work together for the common good, promote solidarity, and seek common interests for survival. This is a requirement of the times, a hope of people worldwide, and an essential aspect of the UN's role.

A "shared future for humanity" is the ideological foundation and spiritual pillar of desert greening. Under the UN's coordination, we must transcend borders, regardless of the size, wealth, system, or historical grievances of countries to address climate change. Land is not divided into north and south, east and west, Asia, Africa, America, Europe, and Australia. People are not divided by gender, skin color, ethnicity, ideology, values, religious beliefs, or partisan affiliations. Resources are not divided among countries. Wealthy nations can donate money, while others can contribute their expertise or share resources with other countries. We must work together to improve the global ecological environment, combat global warming, and secure the survival of future generations.

Global desertification control is a beacon of hope that steers us in the right direction amid chaos and confusion.

Resolving crises is always better than passively accepting them. It is always better to utilize natural resources than wasting them, and harnessing solar energy can benefit humanity. Action is always better than inaction, and early action is more effective than late action. The journey ahead may be filled with challenges, but humans share a common destiny — the basis for uniting people across the world. The future is bright, and humanity's wish to build a beautiful home on Earth will be realized.

There is an increase in one-way heat transfer in the

atmosphere. Only new deserts transfer additional heat to the atmosphere every year. However, we have yet to control desertification to reduce the heat transferred to the atmosphere, resulting in rising atmospheric heat and higher temperatures. This subsequently contributes to the acceleration of global warming. We can only attack without defense, and surrender is the inevitable outcome.

The survival crisis caused by intensified global warming is the common enemy of humanity, and survival should be prioritized above all else. Our only choice is uniting and cooperating to reverse and stop global warming, save the Earth, and save ourselves.

Every investment will yield returns as long as we take action. For every $10,000km^2$ of desertification control, we can reduce the heat transferred to the atmosphere by 320 million tons of crude oil equivalent every year. Deserts receive 4 trillion tons of crude oil equivalent of solar heat each year. (31.4 million square kilometers of desert = 1.27 billion tons of crude oil equivalent of heat/year per $10,000km^2$ of desert. Over half of the total heat transferred from the desert surface to the atmosphere = 635 million tons of crude oil equivalent of heat/year per $10,000km^2$ of desert. Afforestation in deserts can cut the heat transferred to the atmosphere by 50%, which is half of 635 = 320 million tons of crude oil equivalent of heat reduction/year per 10,000 square kilometers of desert afforestation). Global desertification control can reduce the heat transferred to the atmosphere by over 1 trillion tons of crude oil equivalent annually, 100 times the amount of carbon-based energy consumed worldwide each year. This heat is significantly greater than the excess heat absorbed by the atmosphere due to global warming, which can control and reverse climate change to ensure humanity's survival on Earth.

IV. Desertification Control of the Sahara Desert

━━━━━━━◆━━━━━━━

(1) Shifting perspectives, building confidence

The Sahara Desert is 4,800 kilometers long and 1,800 kilometers wide, covering a third of the world's total desert area. It is one of the regions with harsh living conditions, and was a swamp and grassland 10,000 years ago. Rock paintings scattered throughout the Sahara reveal its agricultural civilization during that period. As long as there is sufficient freshwater supply and afforestation now, ecological conditions will improve in the Sahara.

Nature always finds its way throughout history, and humanity lacked the ability to resist its power. The thousand-acre artificial forest of Saihanba marks a new chapter, proving that humanity can change the Earth's current state by harnessing the power of nature.

Two-thirds of the world's deserts are located across multiple countries in mid-latitude regions, and are relatively small and dispersed. The United States has 1.8 million square kilometers of desert, while 1.55 million and

1.28 million square kilometers of desert are located in Australia and China, respectively. Global desertification control can be achieved as long as we take action, and countries have the ability to reduce desertification within their borders.

The Sahara Desert is a vast and concentrated area that is daunting. Combating desertification in the Sahara Desert seems like a mirage, a distant goal that is impossible to reach. There is a common perception that we should not even think about greening the Sahara Desert, restricting the possibility of success. We must first dismiss the notion that "desertification control in the Sahara Desert is not possible", and create a new mindset that "the Sahara Desert can be transformed into a Sahara Oasis".

From east to west, the Sahara Desert occupies the entire mid-latitude region of North Africa, with no room for further expansion. The Saihanba forest park demonstrates that sandy soil can be used to build forests with water supply, and deserts can be transformed into oases. As long as the Sahara maintains its size, we can transform it into a large Sahara Oasis through sustained desertification control.

Generating water vapor from forests is critical for transforming deserts. The "spreading effect of the ecosystem" enables limited water resources to be utilized in multiple locations, allowing desert greening to continue and offering hope in combating desertification.

(2) Phased implementation

Food must be eaten one bite at a time, and things must be done one step at a time. Reducing desertification in the boundless Sahara Desert cannot be achieved within a short period. We need to divide the Sahara into smaller areas, similar to the 50 states of the United States. Under the planning of the UN Desertification Control Committee, desertification control in the Sahara should be conducted in phases based on the areas' various conditions.

The Sahara Desert's vast size meant that it is experiencing climate inertia. Dispersed, small-scale and sporadic afforestation cannot overcome the existing climate inertia. Thus, it is essential to pool efforts and resources for afforestation on a large scale.

Based on the available water supply in the desert, afforestation can be conducted in the first batch of areas, with the planting of trees within a certain distance of each section. Within each section, suitable locations can be selected to construct several water transfer pools. Water will then be diverted or pumped into these pools before being transported to water points through a pipeline network to replenish the saplings. Once a section is successful, this area will become green, a forest will emerge, and we will gradually move to the next section. The growth of forests can be maintained when rainfall increases and stabilizes to a certain level, and the amount of water can then be gradually reduced. This allows the surplus water to be used in new afforestation areas, maximizing the "spreading effect" to expand forested areas.

The amount of available freshwater is the decisive factor determining the speed of desertification control. The Congo River is the world's second-largest river, with an annual runoff of 130.26 billion cubic meters. The African terrain slopes from southeast to northwest, facilitating free-flowing water diversion. In addition to diverting 120-140 billion cubic meters/year from the right bank tributary of Ubangi River, water can also be diverted from other tributaries. Water can also be pumped to add the total annual water diversion to 200-220 billion cubic meters, accelerating desert greening.

If conditions allow, we can utilize the Congo River's hydroelectric resources to build dams for generating electricity, storing and pumping water to Central Sahara, significantly reducing the time required for combating desertification.

(3) An immense challenge that also creates wealth opportunities

The best geographic location on Earth is between latitudes 20-40 degrees. The Sahara Desert, located between 20-35 degrees, is the largest area with suitable latitudes on Earth, exceeding the size of the United States, China, and Australia. The land utilization of high-latitude regions is far less than that of the Sahara after desertification control. The favorable latitudinal location will never change, providing a unique advantage. Once artificial forests have been created, rainfall will increase and ecological conditions will improve in the Sahara, becoming a large oasis suitable for living.

The Sahara Desert has a land area of 9 million square kilometers, 300 billion cubic meters of freshwater flowing into the sea and 400 billion tons of crude oil equivalent of solar energy each year. These wasted resources and energy are the raw materials for tree growth. Through afforestation, these low-cost materials can be transformed into forest products that can increase ecological wealth by tenfold.

With thousands of acres of artificial forests, the Saihanba forest farm in China has spent RMB350 million after 55 years of construction. Its resources are worth RMB15.29 billion, with an input-output ratio of 1:43. The Sahara's latitudinal location is better and water supply conditions can also be improved, making it promising to achieve better afforestation outcomes. A tenfold return on investment is expected, along with ecological benefits that are 10 times greater than economic benefits. This will benefit everyone on Earth.

After forests mature, trees will continue to grow naturally. Under the condition of not reducing forest cover and timber reserves, logging can still be conducted in moderation. Through comprehensive planning and balanced control, we can not only grow timber trees, but also other high-value trees. In areas with better temperature conditions and adequate water supply, various tree species can be planted. Areas with over 60% forest cover presents enormous and long-term wealth opportunities. No parties will suffer losses, and all wealth will be transformed from previously unused resources and energy from nature. Droughts and sandstorms will be a thing of the past and humans will gain wealth and a beautiful home on Earth.

In addition to the land for tree growth, there will be a significant amount of land available for developing other industries. With a favorable climate, sufficient rainfall, rich biodiversity, and abundant products, it is a conducive environment for economic development. The Sahara will become a treasure trove of wealth.

(4) Urgent need

Europe and North Africa are separated by the Mediterranean Sea, but exhibit significant differences in natural conditions, economic development levels and other aspects, presenting potential for joint development of the Sahara.

Countries with limited land resources need to utilize new land resources for development. For example, Japan uses a large amount of land to gain benefits. Countries in high-latitude areas need to adjust and optimize land resources in mid-latitude regions. Products that cannot survive in cold regions can be produced in other areas, and people can opt to live elsewhere during winter.

Countries that are far from Europe and Africa need a transport hub to facilitate the exchange and trade of goods. Developing the Sahara Desert represents a major reorganization and optimization of global resource allocation, a significant opportunity for growth.

Humans are willing to leave a lasting legacy, making amends for past exploitation of oil and minerals, which has repercussions for future generations. Creating the Sahara Forest is the most needed legacy we can leave for future generations. Earth needs more lungs to stop climate change, and adding several lungs like the Amazon rainforest will significantly improve the global ecological environment. Desertification control of the Sahara will reduce the heat transferred from the Earth to the atmosphere, and curb global warming.

There is an urgent need for desertification control in the Sahara Desert, which has the best geographical conditions that will drive global economic growth and accelerate socio-economic development in Africa. Humanity will not suffer any losses, but gain significant benefits from nature.

The strong interest in developing the Sahara was not expressed due to a lack of confidence in the past. Once it is developed with visible results, more parties will seize opportunities and share the large economic pie. Desertification control of the Sahara has a powerful economic driving force in the long run.

(5) Mobilizing capital

Everything is difficult at the beginning, and desertification control in the Sahara Desert is no exception.

Turning the Sahara green is an unprecedented undertaking. It requires an astronomical amount of startup capital to harness nature's vast resources and energy for wealth. No country can afford to finance projects of this scale alone. We must mobilize capital to raise sufficient funds.

Economic activities must be conducted in accordance with economic laws, and profit is a powerful driving force. We must mobilize the powerful force of capital and promote the sharing of economic benefits among investors and countries, but the benefits of tackling global warming belong to all of humanity.

The capital for developing the Sahara Desert can be raised from the following aspects:

1. International bidding

Participating countries should pay infrastructure costs based on the size of the development area they wish to invest. They will have the right to develop the area. Basic infrastructure will be built in advance. The Sahara will be segmented into smaller blocks of land, with development progressing in stages. When a block of land is ready for development, it will be open for international bidding. The winning bid will cover the remaining costs of development.

2. Resource allocation fees

Developing the Arabian Desert requires exchanging oil for freshwater. Most of the resource allocation fees will primarily be used to fund the development of the Sahara Desert, while a small portion will go towards facilitating the country's economic development.

3. Taxes

Once forests have been built and forest products are produced, a small percentage of the product output and other non-timber product output will be paid as taxes to the UN Desertification Control Committee to support subsequent desertification control.

4. Charitable funds and donations

The UN Desertification Control Committee should formulate a desertification control plan for the Sahara Desert, dividing the areas for development into batches based on the amount of water available. International bidding will then open once the list of areas for development has been announced. The winning bid will be selected with fairness and impartiality. A joint development agreement will then be signed with the host country and approval will be sought from the UN Desertification Control Committee to start the joint development.

The investing countries should pay annual investment funds to the UN Desertification Control Committee to finance the project before they are gradually repaid. Other funds will be managed and used by the UN Desertification Control Committee, and audited financial statements will be disclosed.

A "one country, two rights" approach will be implemented in the international joint development zones. Sovereignty and jurisdiction will remain unchanged. The right of use and property rights will be shared, promoting joint development and shared benefits. The investing countries and host countries will collaborate based on the principles of peaceful development and mutual benefit. The international community should recognize the special status of international joint development zones. Moreover, the investing countries and host countries can engage in extensive cooperation in the economy, culture, education, and technology, but the principle of non-intervention should be adopted.

The investing countries can have long-term land use rights, provided that the forest cover reaches over 60% in the development zone within a specific period. This condition is vital in ensuring sufficient rainfall for the growth of forests, promoting sustained afforestation and improving the ecological environment. Once global desertification control is completed, the amount of diverted water can be redistributed to improve water supply conditions in desert forests.

This project can be developed independently with the consent of the host countries. Property rights will be shared, with the host countries holding shares by investing in land and local resources, and profits will be shared and determined through negotiations.

Desert greening is an arduous task. However, miracles are created by those who make sacrifices. Apart from regular wages and benefits, workers should be granted personal equity as employees. Linking personal futures to forest development prospects can help mobilize enthusiasm and accelerate afforestation in deserts. Host countries, investors, and workers are contributors and beneficiaries. No party will suffer any losses, providing a solid foundation for cooperation. Specific legal provisions of the "one country, two rights" system should be formulated under the auspices of the UN Climate Change Conference, based on the spirit of protecting the interests of all parties and safeguarding their legal rights. All countries should jointly implement the legal provisions.

Desertification control in the Sahara will require the establishment of multiple ports, railways, and road networks for transportation. To ensure fair use of transportation resources and improve transportation efficiency, the host countries should manage transport capacity to facilitate deployment.

Countries can participate in joint development either as a single investing country or as a group of countries. Individuals can also participate as investors. To facilitate the management of diplomatic affairs, personal investments should be organized within a national framework.

Countries with deserts can also participate in the development of the Sahara Desert, provided that they ensure desertification control within their borders at a specific time frame.

Investments in afforestation differ from investments in other products.

1. High initial afforestation costs, but low subsequent costs

In addition to costs of establishing production facilities, subsequent production of general products requires substantial investments in raw materials, fuel, labor and working capital. In contrast, afforestation requires a high initial investment, but requires less labor and fewer subsequent costs once saplings grow, and natural resources such as water, land, solar energy, and air become raw materials. It represents an investment with long-term benefits.

2. Low-risk investment

Manufacturing of products often yields profits. However, losses can occur due to various factors, and investment carries some degree of risk. Once trees survive in deserts, natural resources such as water, land, solar energy, and air will be transformed into wealth, and this process is irreversible. This ensures sustained wealth, making it a low-risk investment.

Capital investments are spent on manufacturing of material goods for the society thus far, and all products belong to the investors. Investing in the desertification control of the Sahara Desert marks a shift in investment, transforming the investment of material products to ecological products in the form of afforestation. Forests have the intrinsic value of timber products shared by the investing and host countries, but their ecological benefits are 10 times greater and widely shared in society. Thus, this investment plays a greater role in promoting social progress, improving the ecological environment, and addressing global warming. It is the best choice for investors as it benefits everyone, contributes to society, and leaves a legacy for future generations, ensuring capital appreciation and enhancing social and personal values. Everyone has benefited from social progress and scientific development, and should do their part to give back to society, and create a legacy that will inspire future generations. Participating in the development of the Sahara Desert is an act of kindness that resolves the survival crisis of humanity, and a great opportunity to serve the community.

It is the only option for humanity to save itself and future generations.

Countries and individuals with economic capacity are encouraged to invest in development. With billions of people in this world, global capital will create a powerful driving force for desertification control in the Sahara and offer hope in the greening of the Sahara.

The heat transferred from the desert surface to the atmosphere is the primary cause of rising temperatures worldwide. The Sahara Desert, accounting for a third of the global desert area, is the largest and most concentrated region. Compared to other scattered deserts with smaller areas, the Sahara has a greater impact on global warming. Hence, desertification control in the Sahara Desert is of significance.

Water is regenerated every year, while land, solar

energy, and air are perpetual. These resources that can be transformed into wealth are inexhaustible. Global desertification control is a precious opportunity for people to acquire immense wealth, and also a major initiative to fundamentally improve the ecological environment and address global warming.

Is there anything difficult in the world? If you work at it, the difficult will become easy; if you do not work at it, even the easy becomes difficult.

Global desertification control is an unprecedented cooperation project on a global scale, transcending national boundaries, ideologies and political systems, religious beliefs and partisan affiliations, as well as differences in natural conditions and economic disparities. There are no conflicting interests between countries, with benefits shared by everyone on Earth. Global desertification control will gather different countries, social groups, and individuals to work together for the common good, promote solidarity, and jointly seek benefits from nature.

V. Increasing Global Forest Cover

Since the formation of the Earth 4.6 billion years ago, dense forests have grown. Rich vegetation has maintained suitable temperatures for the Earth's surface and atmosphere, allowing nature and the biological world to coexist.

In their pursuit of survival, humans have cleared forests for agriculture and development. Throughout history, rulers have also cut down large swathes of forest to build palaces and mansions. Once lush with forests, China's Loess Plateau has become a barren land.

Large areas of forest have disappeared due to climate change and human activities, leaving behind vast expanses of bare land. This has increased the amount of solar energy transmitted from the ground to the atmosphere, leading to a rise in temperatures. The rising ground temperature further generates hot air that ascends to high altitudes, creating a thermal environment, reducing rainfall and disrupting the existing ecological balance. Meanwhile, forest cover is declining, resulting in environmental degradation and global warming.

Forest cover is a key indicator of environmental

quality. Forests play a vital role in water conservation, soil retention, water vapor evaporation, rainfall increase, carbon sequestration and oxygen release. It further enhances air quality with negative oxygen ions, mitigating wind and sand erosion, regulating the climate, and producing chlorophyll and proteins. All these functions contribute to the improvement of our environment. Studying the forests of Heilongjiang, Japanese forestry experts concluded that forests accounted for over 96% of the total ecological value, while timber and byproducts constituted a mere 3.7%. This highlights the importance of forests, which have a much higher ecological value than timber. Forests are allies and protectors of humanity, while rainfall is needed to produce freshwater essential for human life and productivity. Rainfall would decline and dissipate without forests, resulting in the loss of perennial rivers. In addition, humans cannot live without water. Thus, the lives of humans are inextricably linked to trees. We must protect and foster a love for trees as its contribution to our existence is immeasurable.

Forest cover is a key indicator of environmental quality. While past deforestation data is incomplete, we learned that there were 5.5 billion hectares of forests on Earth in 1862, before dwindling to 2.6 billion hectares in the 1970s — a loss of over 50%. This drastic fall in forest cover diminished the Earth's capacity for carbon sequestration and oxygen release. Hence, the decline in forest cover is a key contributor to global warming.

Apart from extensive afforestation in deserts, similar

tree-planting initiatives should be conducted in non-desert areas with potential for afforestation.

Feeding a global population of 7 billion necessitates sufficient arable land. However, there are currently 1.48 billion hectares of cultivated land, accounting for a mere 11% of the Earth's total land area of 13.39 billion hectares. In contrast, forests and woodlands occupy 30.5% or 4.09 billion hectares of the total land area. Excluding the global desert area of 3.14 billion hectares (23.4% of the total land area), 35% of land is available for afforestation and development. Utilizing a portion of this land for afforestation could increase global forest cover to over 40%.

Grassland is 2.5 times larger than cultivated areas, but with a lower tree population. Young trees struggle to survive and grow in these areas due to livestock grazing.

With robust root systems that penetrate deep into the soil, trees have better water absorption and storage, enhancing their survival rates. Conversely, grass with shallow roots are less efficient at water absorption and storage, rendering them more vulnerable. Consequently, forests contribute more to environmental improvement and climate change mitigation than grasslands. Afforestation in China's Saihanba forest park has resulted in an 18-fold increase in water conservation capacity in its city of Chengde. Afforestation in grasslands would significantly enhance water conservation, boost forage yield, increase livestock production, and bolster resilience against natural disasters. Reliant on natural conditions for survival, grasslands feature low output and land utilization rates. On the other hand, artificial grasslands can provide substantial quantities of high-quality fodder on smaller land areas, boosting livestock production.

Some 300-450 livestock unit per hectare of artificial grassland are harvested in New Zealand, the Netherlands, the UK, and Germany (one unit equates to a 1kg weight gain in a fattening cattle). In contrast, natural grasslands can only harvest 20-30 livestock units per hectare, a stark difference of 10 to 15 times.

The prevalence of artificial grasslands serves as an indicator of a country or region's development level of animal husbandry in grasslands. The Netherlands has converted its natural grasslands to artificial ones, feeding its dairy cattle with green fodder. Meanwhile, artificial and semi-natural grasslands constitute 66% of New Zealand's total grassland area.

Developing artificial grasslands through dense forests enhances soil water retention, promotes grass growth, and increases livestock yield.

Developed countries with a robust livestock sector are using innovative technologies to boost output. The Dutch livestock sector is dominated by family farms and their operations have expanded as a result of mechanized agriculture. In 1987, there were an average of 410 pigs, 27,300 broilers, 8,400 hens, 40 dairy cows, and 258 fattening calves. Expanding the scale of operations facilitates the implementation of livestock technology, promotes mechanized and mass production, and increases livestock yield.

To effectively utilize large swathes of low-yield grassland, a "three-model strategy" can be implemented. One-third of grasslands can be developed into artificial grasslands to increase fodder yield, another one-third can be allocated to afforestation for ecological improvement, and the remaining one-third can be used for mechanized farming of crops such as corn, oats, and starchy vegetables, which are used as high-quality feed to raise more livestock. This integration of forestry, agriculture, and animal husbandry would optimize grassland utilization and significantly increase livestock production.

Developing animal husbandry necessitates a shift from nomadic and free-range farming practices to confined livestock systems. This change is crucial to limit the damage of grazing animals on young trees and grasslands.

However, maintaining sufficient arable land remains paramount as the global population continues to rise. Innovative solutions are needed to address the competition for land between agriculture and forestry. Chestnuts, known as a "grains that grow on trees", offer a promising solution as it can thrive in arid and infertile conditions, making it suitable for cultivation across various areas. Chestnuts are high in starch, protein, fat, vitamins, and minerals. With proper management, the grafting of chestnut trees can bear fruit within two to three years, with a peak yield of

600-800kg per 0.06 hectare in three to four years. A century-old chestnut tree can produce dozens of kilograms of fruit in a year, and cultivating chestnuts requires minimal labor compared to other crops.

Planting and growing chestnuts can address food security concerns without expanding cultivated land, while simultaneously enhancing forest cover.

Furthermore, high-value trees, fruits, nuts, oil crops, medicinal plants, tea, and mulberry can also be developed to generate economic benefits, as well as diversify product offerings to enhance the quality of life.

Mountainous regions make up roughly 15% of the world's total land area – larger than the 11% occupied by arable land – are generally not suitable for cultivation. This means that there is no competition for land use between mountainous regions and arable land, making them ideal locations for forest development. Most mountainous terrains can be used to build forests, except some rocky peaks. Mountain forests act as vital water conservation and regulation zones, functioning as natural reservoirs. The pristine forests of the Alps are vital to the Danube river, a major economic artery for many European nations. Expanding forest cover in mountainous areas holds significant potential for economic growth, ecological improvement, and climate regulation.

Building forests in farmlands can also increase forest cover, enhance soil water retention, improve ecological conditions, boost yield, and strengthen resilience against natural disasters such as floods, thereby benefiting agricultural production.

Increasing the forest cover to over 40% of the world's total land area (excluding the polar regions) holds the key to combating global warming, mitigating existential threats, improving the ecological environment, and building livable environments.

The UN Climate Change Conference should establish a specific agency or organization responsible for increasing global forest cover. A comprehensive global plan should be formulated to increase forest cover, with different targets and timelines based on the regions' natural environment and economic conditions. The UN should also urge all countries to implement these plans accordingly.

This call to increase global forest cover can mobilize every nation and individual to plant trees in the fight against climate change.

VI. Climate Revolution

The year 2022 marked the start of the human survival crisis, a turning point in history. With Earth transitioning from a warm to a hot planet, humanity faces an era of unprecedented peril.

In 2022, the Northern Hemisphere grappled with severe drought and extreme heat. Record temperatures were reported in North America, Europe, the Mediterranean, East and North Africa, and South China, while the western part of United States experienced its most serious drought in 1,200 years. Dr. Hartmann of the Potsdam Institute for Climate Impact Research said, "We have had five consecutive years of drought, and this year is the worst pan-European drought in centuries". Droughts trigger a surge in forest fires, earthquakes, volcanic eruptions and typhoons. The combined effects of drought and dying of forests have drastically reduced river flow. In China's Wuhan, the Yangtze River's water level plummeted by 42% in August. Drought and heat have unleashed a cascade of ecological devastation.

Meanwhile, temperatures in Spain reached 39 to 45 degrees Celsius, with the heat killing 510 people as of July 18, 2022. In many places such as India, temperatures have already hit 50 degrees Celsius. Temperatures above 50 degrees Celsius are becoming increasingly common as global warming intensifies and atmospheric heat continues to rise. Temperatures could rise even further to 55, 60, or even 65 degrees Celsius in the future. The areas affected by such heatwaves are expanding, and with increased intensity and frequency. How will people live under such conditions?

The accelerating melting of glaciers, including a 60 billion ton iceberg collapsing off Greenland, exacerbates the climate crisis. About 210,000 glaciers provide freshwater to 2 billion people worldwide. Studies indicate that nearly half of these glaciers will vanish by the end of this century, transforming river basins into deserts and wastelands. China's Xinjiang faces a grim future as it is entirely reliant on meltwater from the Tianshan Mountains. The melting of these glaciers would transform Xinjiang into a new desert, accelerating desertification throughout north China. The emergence of these new deserts would amplify heat transfer to the atmosphere, escalating global warming and creating a vicious cycle. As the atmosphere at high altitudes continues to warm, the Earth's surface temperature will inevitably rise, pushing us closer to an extremely hot planet. Humanity's survival hinges on taking decisive action. Without intervention, our species faces extinction within the next 200-400 years. This is not an alarmist prediction, but a future reality based on current trends. Luke Kemp, a researcher at the Centre for the Study of Existential Risk at the University of Cambridge, said, "Yes, I think human extinction is plausible".

Combating global warming requires a shift in our approach. We must shift our focus on greenhouse gases and take a comprehensive strategy based on the three recommended measures. Global desertification control, increasing global forest cover, as well as energy conservation and emission reduction must be implemented in tandem, addressing both natural and human factors that contribute to rising atmospheric temperatures. Only through this comprehensive approach can we curb global warming and avert the human survival crisis. Global desertification control is paramount among the three strategic measures.

(1) Main Cause of Global Warming

The disproportionate distribution of heat radiated by solar energy to the Earth is the main cause of global warming. The Earth's surface absorbs and utilizes too little solar radiation, while the atmosphere absorbs excess heat. This imbalance is caused by the interplay between mid-latitude deserts and mid-latitude westerly winds. This interaction contributes to an annual expansion of global desert area by $60,000 km^2$, releasing heat equivalent to 3.8 billion tons of crude oil to the atmosphere each year. This rising heat is the main driving force of accelerating global warming that pushes humanity towards extinction.

Excess atmospheric heat is the main problem of global warming, which involves a massive amount of heat equivalent to trillions of tons of crude oil each year. However, carbon dioxide does not produce additional heat. Therefore, we must first identify the source of this heat.

Deserts transfer heat to the atmosphere at a rate that is more than double that of areas with high forest cover. Deserts release most of the absorbed solar radiation back into the atmosphere as heat, making them a major contributor to rising atmospheric temperatures and global warming.

Deserts, which account for a quarter of the world's total land area, receive a staggering amount of solar radiation. Based on the solar radiation data of 5,000-6,400 MJ/m2 per year in Xinjiang, the world's deserts receive solar energy equivalent to 3.9 to 5.07 trillion tons of crude oil each year. Of this figure, over 2 trillion tons are transferred to the atmosphere. In terms of heat balance, the world currently consumes nearly 10 billion tons of crude oil equivalent of carbon-based energy in a year, and releases less than 4 billion tons of crude oil equivalent of heat to the atmosphere. Thus, the amount of heat transmitted from deserts to the atmosphere is 500 times greater than heat released from fuel combustion. Focusing solely on energy conservation and emission reduction, which only contributes to 0.2% of the total heat release to the atmosphere, while overlooking the 99.8% of heat release contributed by global deserts, is futile in tackling global warming.

The harsh conditions of deserts prevent the creation of natural ecosystems, hindering the absorption and utilization of solar energy. Consequently, a large amount of solar radiation is released back into the atmosphere as heat, driving global warming. To combat this, we must implement effective measures to harness freshwater resources for afforestation in deserts. Establishing new, self-sustaining ecosystems that can generate water vapor would enable the absorption of solar radiation, naturally reducing the heat transmitted to the atmosphere. Afforestation in deserts holds the key to regulating the distribution of solar heat on Earth.

China's Saihanba forest park is testament to the transformative power of afforestation. This man-made forest spanning thousands of acres is the world's largest artificial forest. It represents a green miracle of transforming wasteland into forests and is a successful experiment in planting trees on sandy soil. The fact that the forests are growing in Saihanba over the past 60 years is a strong indication that artificial forests can survive on sandy soil. The park currently has a forest cover of over 80%. For this reason, the United Nations Environment Programme awarded the Saihanba forest farm as Champion of the Earth. The economic value of the Saihanba forest farm is 43 times of its initial cost, proving that afforestation in deserts can convert wasted resources and energy into wealth.

Forests improve ecological functions such as water conservation, soil retention, rainfall increase, carbon sequestration and oxygen release, wind and sand erosion mitigation, climate regulation, and the production of chlorophyll and proteins. Studying the forests of Heilongjiang, Japanese forestry experts concluded that forests accounted for over 96% of the total ecological value, while timber and byproducts make up a mere 3.7%. This underscores the ecological significance of forests that far outweighs the value of timber.

There were 5.5 billion hectares of forests in 1862, but global forest cover plummeted to 2.6 billion hectares in the 1970s, leading to a substantial increase in heat transmitted from the Earth's surface to the atmosphere. This decline in forest cover is a key contributor to global warming.

Forests are allies and protectors of humanity, while rainfall is needed to produce freshwater essential for human life and food production. Rainfall would decline and dissipate without forests, resulting in the loss of perennial rivers. Moreover, humans would cease to exist without water. Thus, the lives of humans are inextricably linked to trees. We owe a great debt to trees for our very existence. Humanity and trees share a common destiny, coexisting within a "community of shared future". As global warming accelerates, prolonged and increasingly severe heat, drought, and forest fires threaten to destroy the environment, ultimately leading to our demise.

Global desertification control and increasing global forest cover are a two-pronged strategy to protect our living spaces through afforestation. By addressing the root causes of climate change, these measures help mitigate rising temperatures, reduce extreme weather events, and minimize natural disasters. They enhance rainfall, improve ecological conditions and build livable environments, helping us overcome the human survival crisis. These two strategies have carbon sequestration and oxygen release functions that are hundreds of times greater than those of energy conservation and emission reduction alone.

Global desertification control, increasing global forest cover, as well as energy conservation and emission reduction complement one another to address the natural and human causes of rising atmospheric temperatures. Global desertification control is the foundation of the three strategic measures, while increasing global forest cover consolidates and complements the effectiveness of global desertification control.

The power of nature is immense, while the power of humans is minuscule by comparison. Our only viable path of combating climate change is using human intelligence to harness the power of nature.

The debate over whether deserts or carbon dioxide are the main contributors to global warming reflects a major difference in understanding climate change.

Attributing the main cause of global warming from carbon emissions to global desertification represents a revolutionary change in understanding.

It must be acknowledged that carbon emissions contribute to global warming, but they are not the main cause. Attributing the main cause to carbon emissions obscures the true culprit – global desertification – which transmits an additional 3.8 billion tons of crude oil worth of solar heat into the atmosphere, pushing us closer to ecological collapse and human extinction.

While energy conservation and emissions reduction has achieved success to a certain extent, these accomplishments are insignificant as they do not involve a broader, comprehensive strategy that includes other crucial measures. The progress made in cutting emissions seems negligible compared to the harm caused by obscuring the true culprit, and misconceptions that could ultimately lead to the destruction of humankind.

(2) The Human Survival Crisis Exists

A "normal temperature" is below 45 degrees Celsius, which is suitable for human survival, but humans cannot live with an extremely hot temperature above 50 degrees Celsius. Accelerated global warming is a manifestation of the transformation from a "normal temperature" to an "extremely hot temperature, indicating that the human survival crisis exists.

Solar heat can benefit, but also destroy humanity. Whether it benefits or destroys depends on how people treat deserts. Reducing desertification to limit the amount of solar heat can benefit humanity. On the other hand, allowing deserts to increase and expand will cross ecological redlines and destroy humanity through global warming. Hence, desertification control determines whether deserts benefit or destroy humanity.

When deserts expand from the current 31.4 million square kilometers to 40 million square kilometers, the heat transferred to the atmosphere will increase from an equivalent 2-2.4 trillion tons of crude oil to 2.5-3.04 trillion tons. This will increase its power of destroying ecological conditions. It takes about 100 years for deserts to increase from 31.4 million square kilometers to 40 million square kilometers, and the peak of the survival crisis is just a matter of time.

Excess atmospheric heat is the main problem of global warming. The uneven distribution of solar heat will inevitably lead to an uneven distribution of precipitation between land and ocean. Heat is rising in the atmosphere, the heat range of the thermal environment is increasing at high altitudes, and most land areas are like deserts with similar thermal environments. Rainfall will decline due to decreased water vapor at high altitudes, and rain will only fall over low-temperature oceans to become seawater. Precipitation on land will lessen, while regular droughts and high temperatures will become the norm. When rainfall drops to below 300mm, trees will dry up and die, river flow will be disrupted, food production will be affected, and tens of millions of people will starve to death.

Temperatures will inevitably rise to 50 degrees Celsius or above as the heat in the atmosphere increases. Plagues and viruses will break out, and hell will descend on Earth.

Mid-latitude deserts interact with airflows in a westerly high-altitude current to expand the size and number of deserts. If this continues, human extinction is inevitable. The greatest danger lies in not being able to see the danger. Humanity must save itself by fighting against desertification, as this is the only solution. Disaster is not an illusion or speculation, but based on real data.

The relationship between human survival and extinction, as well as atmospheric heat can be illustrated with a graph:

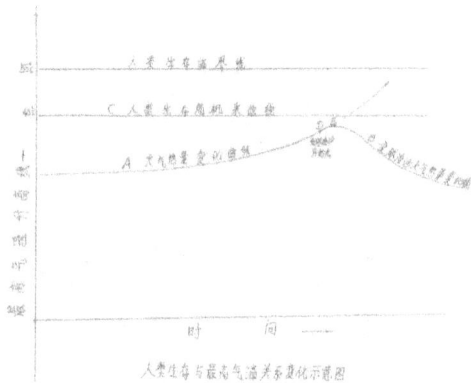

人类生存与最高气温关系变化示意图

Curve A: The global annual increase in deserts is 60,000km^2, and the annual rise in heat release to the atmosphere is equivalent to 3.8 billion tons of crude oil. Global warming will intensify, deserts will gradually expand from 60,000km^2 to 150,000km^2, and the amount of heat transmitted to the atmosphere may reach an equivalent of 9.4 billion tons of crude oil. The atmospheric heat change curve will gradually increase and move upward. It will inevitably intersect with the human survival threshold, and humans will gradually go extinct due to extreme heat.

Curve B: Atmospheric heat change curve after global

desertification control. The curve shows that global desertification control starts from point D, reducing the heat transferred from the ground to the atmosphere, and changing the direction of curve A from an upward trend to a flat and slightly downward trajectory. From points D to E, the annual average afforestation area is still less than the annual increase in desert area, with the curve rising slightly. After point E, the annual afforestation area is larger than the annual desert area increase, with a descending curve before transitioning to a flat line. This suggests that human survival is possible as the atmospheric heat change curve is below the human survival crisis line.

The graph further indicates that humans will eventually perish without global desertification control. Conversely, humanity can save itself after reducing desertification.

(3) Time is of the Essence

Executing the three strategic measures is a monumental and challenging task, but they must be implemented within a specific time frame to be effective.

Sufficient freshwater supply is essential for afforestation in deserts. However, freshwater resources that can be used for desertification control are limited. China's desertification control project involves water diversion from Tibet's Yarlung Zangbo River, which is 5,000km away. As global warming intensifies, droughts and high temperatures become increasingly severe and frequent, causing drying trees, decreasing river flows, and reducing the amount of freshwater available for diversion. This subsequently limits the area available for afforestation and makes desertification control increasingly difficult. Moreover, glaciers are melting faster than ever, while deserts and barren land are increasing rapidly. Deserts are expected to gradually expand from the current $60,000km^2$ to $110,000km^2$. When the area of deserts is larger than the desert area that humans managed to reduce through afforestation, the expansion of deserts will become irreversible. In other words, global desertification control will be ineffective, and humans will be unable to avoid its fate of extinction. Thus, seizing the opportunity to implement global desertification control within a specific time frame will determine the fate of humanity. The world must take action now, planting trees every year to reduce desert areas, gradually curbing global warming, and ensuring human survival. There is still hope for humanity.

There is only a short time span of a few decades for global desertification control to be effective. Time is of the essence, and opportunities do not come by easily. Missing the opportunity to act now means an impending survival crisis — a slow suicide for humanity.

Global desertification control is scientifically proven to be effective. Every $10,000km^2$ of afforestation in deserts can reduce 320 million tons of crude oil equivalent of heat transferred to the atmosphere each year.

The Arab region, the United States, and China are

currently the only territories with the economic means to implement desertification control. China and the United States have the will to tackle global warming. The Arab region has 2.33 million square kilometers of deserts, while the United States and China have 1.8 million and 1.28 million square kilometers of deserts, respectively. Reducing desertification in these three areas can cut the annual amount of heat transfer to the atmosphere equivalent to 173.1 billion tons of crude oil, which is 17 times the total annual consumption of carbon-based energy in the world. Forest area will expand by an average of $130,000$-$150,000 km^2$ every year if desertification is reduced in these three areas within 35-40 years. This means that the forest area will be larger than desert areas that expand $60,000$ to $80,000 km^2$ each year. Reducing desertification will reverse the accelerating trend of global warming.

This is of great significance because it starts to limit the effects of global warming, and humans can escape the survival crisis to continue global desertification control efforts. This is a turning point in the future and fate of humanity. Seizing the opportunity to reduce the desert area now will determine the success of combating desertification and pave the way for future global desertification control.

Dispelling concerns, pessimism, and reluctance, while instilling hope and expectations of success will motivate the world to implement desertification control measures. Valuable experience will ensure the smooth progress of the project, accelerating the speed of reducing desert areas, and ultimately eliminating deserts that are the root cause of global warming.

To ensure human survival, necessary measures can be taken to accelerate desertification control. Using China as an example, water was diverted from Tibet to Xinjiang to reduce desertification, allowing afforestation to be conducted and attracting private capital through preferential policies for sustainable land use. Through various business activities, the state can mobilize private capital and promote confidence among investors. Dozens of forest farms can be built to speed up desertification control and multiple approaches can be taken to solve the problem of raising a large amount of funds.

(4) Establishing a New International Order

The emergence of humanity, from families, clans, tribes, localities, regions, to nations, gradually formed an international order based on power and interests. This is an international order characterized by the survival of the fittest, where the strong will survive and the weak will die. The modern industrial revolution promoted the rapid development of the manufacturing industry and transportation, and an hegemonic world order emerged.

World orders in the past were established on the basis that natural conditions adapted to the survival and development of humanity, and natural conditions did not interfere with the establishment of the international order.

The record-breaking droughts and temperatures in the

Northern Hemisphere in 2022 marked the beginning of the transformation from a normal temperature to an extremely hot temperature. Global warming will intensify year by year, while droughts and high temperatures will become more severe and frequent. Natural ecological conditions began to change from adapting to human survival and development to being unsuitable for human survival and development. The survival crisis of humanity has arrived. Everything will be destroyed when humans face extinction, be it hegemony, wealth, interests, ideologies, values, religious beliefs and partisan affiliations, science, culture or civilization. Nothing is left without the ability to survive. "We must cooperate to coexist, as conflict leads to destruction." The right to survival is above all else.

Atmospheric heat determines the direction and trend of global warming. The interaction between mid-latitude deserts and airflows in a westerly high-altitude current determines the increase of atmospheric heat, raising the risk of human extinction. The Earth has formed a terrifying force of self-destruction. It is similar to sailing against the current. One will fall behind if they do not advance. Long-term ignorance and inaction have brought humanity to the brink of a survival crisis. Humanity must save itself, not only by counteracting the increase in atmospheric heat, but also making efforts to reduce the existing atmospheric heat. This challenging task means that humans must double their efforts to survive.

There is an urgent need to mobilize people and countries to implement desertification control measures now. Reducing desertification control is an enormous undertaking that no one country can shoulder this responsibility. Under the auspices of the UN, we must mobilize everyone to accelerate its progress. The shift from "internal fighting" to "collective rescue" will be a turning point and liberation for humanity. It will promote the establishment of a new international order based on equality, cooperation, and mutual benefits.

Without conflict of interests among nations, the UN can play a leading role in global desertification control. We must choose bold and capable leaders who have a good understanding of the danger and urgency of the survival crisis.

The human survival crisis is a catastrophe for all, including Americans, and is thousands of times greater than the 9/11 attacks. We must unite to fight against our enemy and immediately shift from the struggle for hegemony to "collective rescue". China can take the lead in "collective rescue" with its experience in Saihanba forest park. On the other hand, the United States should change its policy of containing China, and stop its interference over Taiwan and the South China Sea. With a peaceful and stable world, China can accelerate its project of diverting water from Tibet to Xinjiang, manage its deserts, and lead global desertification control efforts to ensure human survival. It is the hope of the world population that China can be a good leader. China's development is a blessing, and not a threat to the world.

The enemy is not humans from other countries, but global warming that will destroy humanity. Human extinction is not an illusion or speculation, but the inevitable consequence of desert expansion. It teaches us to be clear-headed, distinguish between friends and foes, cooperate for coexistence, and fight against destruction.

There are still politicians and interest groups who are still keen on maintaining hegemony and accumulating wealth. They spare no effort to contain, suppress, block, provoke, sabotage, smear, create "threat theories", and instigate wars. They are willing to kill imaginary enemies even if it means self-destruction. By doing so, they reduce humanity's capacity to deal with the survival crisis, prevent response measures, shorten the effective response time frame, and accelerate the arrival of the survival crisis. This is unwise behavior with a lack of foresight. Enemies want to destroy humanity, calling themselves hegemonic warriors and elites, but are in fact fools who harm themselves and others, driving humans to extinction.

It is never too late to mend. It is hoped that these people can clear their minds, change their perspectives, give up their obsession with hegemony, and join the cause to save humanity and future generations.

VII. Theoretical Discussion on

Curbing Global Warming

Curbing and reversing global warming, as well as resolving the survival crisis are major issues facing humanity.

Both natural and anthropogenic factors contribute to lobal warming. There are two types of natural factors — one that humans cannot change, such as atmospheric circulation and latitudinal temperature differences. The other involves natural factors that humans can change, such as ecological environment conditions.

Atmospheric circulation has a major impact on climate, but the formation of atmospheric circulation is beyond human control, such as the centrifugal force of the Earth's rotation, as well as the Earth's gravitational force between the polar regions and other areas. Atmospheric circulation has existed for a long time, and it has been proven that atmospheric circulation does not pose a threat to human survival. Thus, we will not discuss atmospheric circulation since its effect on climate change is beyond our control and does not pose a threat to humanity. We will focus on the impact of natural factors that humans can change, such as ecological environment conditions on global warming.

Theories of curbing global warming are relatively new and have begun to attract people's attention. These theories involve multiple disciplines, such as geography, geology, meteorology, ecology, environmental protection, resources, energy, water conservation, hydrology, agriculture, and forestry. It is a comprehensive study of nature, which requires a broad knowledge base linking different disciplines. This is beneficial for understanding the laws of nature, using natural forces for the benefit of humanity and tackling global warming.

The development of science has progressed from the macro to micro level, with different branches, disciplines, and specializations being studied in detail, promoting the progress of human civilization. This is moving in the right direction, but everything has two sides. While it has advantages, there are also adverse effects. Dividing nature into different branches, disciplines, and specializations has blurred the understanding of nature and the intrinsic link of various natural phenomena. The bias between micro and macro research, and lack of comprehensive studies on nature are shortcomings in academic research. As a result, there are still insufficient studies and solutions on major issues such as global warming. To raise awareness on this issue, my personal thoughts and opinions will be discussed and all ideas, suggestions and criticisms are welcome. I hope to discuss different viewpoints and perspectives to propose effective measures in reversing global warming.

(1) Earth's heat balance determines global warming

Solar energy, the most abundant energy source on Earth, provides the power needed for the movement of all things.

Nature is composed of countless equilibrium systems that are closely related to human survival, such as the water cycle, carbon cycle, and oxygen cycle. These equilibrium systems are controlled and governed by the solar energy-Earth heat balance. Heat balance is the theoretical basis for studying natural phenomena and global warming.

According to the solar energy-Earth heat balance diagram, 81% of the solar heat is absorbed by the Earth's surface and released to the atmosphere. The amount of heat transferred from desert surfaces to the atmosphere is more than double that of the heat transmitted from the ground of forests to the atmosphere. It is precisely this heat with higher than normal temperatures released from desert surfaces to the atmosphere that raises temperatures and accelerates global warming.

The solar energy-Earth heat balance diagram also shows that water vapor and carbon dioxide in the atmosphere can absorb most of the heat, playing a role in thermal insulation and reducing energy consumption. It is unrealistic to place high expectations on cutting carbon emissions to tackle warming as this can only control the atmospheric heat absorption to some extent.

A source of heat is needed for temperatures to rise. Carbon dioxide in the atmosphere does not generate heat, so where does the heat that increases atmospheric temperatures come from? From the heat balance diagram, the heat that increases atmospheric temperatures is produced from the extreme solar heat transferred from the surface to the atmosphere. Hence, reducing the heat transmitted from the surface to the atmosphere is key in combating global warming. According to the radiation heat transfer theory, the intensity of heat radiation emitted by body is proportional to the fourth power of the body's absolute temperature. This means that radiation heat transfer is dependent on the absolute temperature.

$Q = \sigma \times A \times (T1^4 - T2^4)$

Q - Radiation heat transfer

σ - Radiation heat transfer coefficient

A - Surface area of body

$T1^4$ - Fourth power of the heat transfer body's absolute temperature

$T2^4$ - Fourth power of the heat-receiving body's absolute temperature

The atmosphere is the heat-receiving body, which will not be discussed. However, there is a big difference in heat transfer between the desert surface and forest floor in deserts. The temperature of the desert surface is only 32-28 degrees higher than the forest floor in deserts, but its absolute temperature to the fourth power is one-third higher. This means that deserts transfer more heat to the atmosphere. In addition, most of the heat absorbed by desert surfaces is then re-transmitted to the atmosphere in the form of rising hot air. Therefore, the sum of these two parts of heat transferred to the atmosphere accounts for over half of the solar heat received by the desert surface. In other words, afforestation in deserts can reduce more than half of the heat transmitted from deserts to the atmosphere. Reducing the temperature difference in heat transfer between the desert surface and forest floor in deserts will resolve the issue of excess heat transfer from deserts to the atmosphere.

Temperature variation is also the driving force of climate change. Oceans make up two-thirds of the Earth's surface, with land accounting for the remaining one-third. Oceans need to absorb a lot of heat (heat of vaporization is 580kcal/kg) to evaporate a large amount of water vapor, thus cooling the ocean surface and air above it to form a lower temperature zone. On the other hand, less water vapor evaporates on land, resulting in lower absorption of heat and higher ground temperatures. Temperatures are lower on ocean surfaces, and higher on land surfaces with the same amount of solar heat, forming a large temperature variation between the ocean and land and monsoon winds flowing from oceans towards land. Moreover, there are also large temperature differences between deserts and other areas, as well as deserts and forests on land. Day-night temperature differences, topographical and geographical temperature differences further exacerbate global warming. Reducing these temperature variations can stop climate change. Afforestation is also effective in reducing temperature differences between land and ocean surfaces. The planting of more trees will result in fewer disasters, while fewer trees will lead to more disasters.

The effect of temperature differences on climate change is worsening. Temperatures at the higher range will have a greater impact on global warming. For example, it does not feel too hot at 30-34 degrees Celsius during summer, but at 37-40 degrees Celsius will feel unbearably hot. High temperatures over desert areas are the largest contributor to global warming. Desertification control is vital in tackling climate change as deserts are where high atmospheric temperatures are produced and the main source of heat for global warming.

Apart from the three strategic measures of desertification control, improving forest cover and reducing energy consumption and emissions, curbing and reversing global warming require us to address the natural and anthropogenic factors contributing to rising temperatures.

Ground temperatures will not rise even though forests in deserts can transfer most of the heat from the desert surface to the forest floor. This heat is absorbed and utilized by the evaporation of water vapor and photosynthesis of trees for energy flow and material cycle of the ecosystem, promoting the development and growth of ecosystems.

Solar radiation transfers heat to Earth, and the ground

absorbs heat before transmitting to the atmosphere. As long as the ground absorbs more heat, there will be less heat for the atmosphere. Therefore, making the ground absorb as much heat as possible is the key to reducing heat transfer to the atmosphere.

The Earth's heat balance determines global warming. This is a theoretical basis for understanding climate change and determines the direction and measures taken to address global warming. It is also a major issue related to the ecological Earth and fate of humanity.

Discussions on combating global warming currently focus on reducing energy consumption and carbon emissions, while global desertification control is not considered as an option. The carbon balance theory is used to replace the heat balance theory. These are two ways of thinking, two different directions and two varying measures that eventually produce two different outcomes in mitigating the effects of global warming. This is a major issue that should be addressed first in tackling global warming.

Excess atmospheric heat is the main problem of global warming. It determines the direction and trend of global warming, changes in ecological conditions, and the extent of damage to the ecological environment. The carbon balance theory posits that atmospheric heat is naturally formed and cannot be changed by humans. In contrast, the heat balance theory believes that atmospheric heat can be controlled,   transferred,   and   transformed   through afforestation in deserts. Atmospheric heat can only be controlled and regulated to a certain extent.

According to the carbon balance theory, human-driven activities caused the increase in carbon emissions that contribute to global warming, while natural causes were not a factor. In fact, the impact of natural factors is hundreds of times greater than that of human factors. Overlooking natural factors will have disastrous consequences. Treating the secondary cause as the primary cause, or a minor problem as the biggest problem, and proposing the reduction of energy consumption and emissions as the only solution will lead us to the wrong direction in resolving global warming.

(2) An Appropriate Heat Distribution Ratio is Required

To date, Earth is the only planet in the universe with life, earning the title of ecological environment. Apart from basic conditions such as water, air, and solar energy, the ecological environment must also have an appropriate heat distribution ratio between the ground and atmosphere.

The Earth's heat balance determines global warming, requiring an appropriate proportion of heat distribution. To ensure the Earth's ecological conditions are suitable for the survival and development of living organisms, an appropriate solar heat distribution ratio and balance point for heat distribution are needed. If the proportion of heat distributed to the atmosphere is higher than the balance point, the ecological conditions that were previously ideal for the survival of life will become unsuitable. For example, land precipitation will shift to the ocean and desertification will expand, transforming the ecological environment into a non-ecological Earth, and humanity will no longer be able to live on Earth.

The size of deserts is the biggest factor affecting the solar heat distribution ratio on Earth. There are no ecosystems to absorb solar heat at deserts, thus most of the heat is transferred back to the atmosphere. The amount of heat transmitted from the desert surface to the atmosphere is more than twice that of the forest floor.

At the beginning of Earth's formation 4.6 billion years ago, there were only a small number of deserts. This was a period when the proportion of solar heat transferred to the atmosphere was below the balance point, where the ground absorbed more heat and the atmosphere absorbed less heat. Earth's ecological conditions have always been conducive to the growth of living organisms, resulting in the emergence of humans on Earth millions of years ago. This also led humans to take their survival on Earth for granted.

The interaction between deserts and airflows in a westerly high-altitude current has resulted in the expansion of deserts, and the amount of solar heat transferred to the atmosphere has been increasing year by year. This has led to the acceleration of global warming. After thousands of years of development, the proportion of heat transferred to the atmosphere is close to the balance point. The heat distribution ratio is expected to surpass the balance point when global warming intensifies, damaging ecological conditions and transforming the ecological environment. Deserts currently increase 60,000km^2 in size each year, and the annual increase in heat transferred to the atmosphere is equivalent to 3.8 billion tons of crude oil. Thus, we are already heading towards breaking through the balance point. The world needs to mobilize and implement desertification control measures now, plant trees to decrease the desert area, and reduce the heat transferred from the desert surface to the atmosphere. We should maintain the heat distribution ratio below the balance point, or lower the amount of heat transmitted to the atmosphere as much as possible.

The planting of trees in every 10,000km^2 of desert can reduce the amount of heat transferred to the atmosphere equivalent to 320 million tons of crude oil every year. Afforestation in deserts is the most effective way to reduce heat transfer to the atmosphere.

The proportion of heat transferred to the atmosphere from solar heat reaching the Earth's surface has reached 34%. Record droughts and high temperatures were reported in the Northern Hemisphere in 2022 and 2023. These conditions will continue to worsen and become the norm. Many signs of damage to existing ecological conditions have emerged, indicating that the proportion of heat transferred from the ground to the atmosphere has reached 34%. The balance point is estimated at 35-36%. Once this balance point is breached, ecological conditions will deteriorate.

The proposed balance point has the following implications:

1. Boundary Line

The boundary line for the appropriate heat distribution ratio between the ground and atmosphere on Earth also represents the ecological redline. The atmosphere will absorb too much heat once this redline is crossed, accelerating global warming and gradually destroying the Earth's ecological conditions. Ultimately, it will lead to the disappearance of Earth's ecological environment, and humanity will cease to exist. The most important task for humanity now is to spare no effort in ensuring that the atmospheric heat does not cross the redline and reduce the proportion of solar heat transferred to the atmosphere to below 35-36%. This is the only way for future generations to survive on Earth.

2. Sounding the Alarm

The proportion of solar heat distributed to the atmosphere has reached 34%, close to the balance point of 35-36%. Global warming is accelerating, and the human survival crisis is looming. We must take urgent action to implement desertification control measures, and save the ecological environment to save humanity.

3. Global Desertification Control is Urgent

The size of deserts has the biggest impact on Earth's heat distribution ratio.

Desert surfaces transfer more than twice the amount of solar heat than forest floors. Afforestation in deserts plays a significant role in changing the proportion of solar heat distribution between the ground and atmosphere. In other words, more heat is transmitted to the atmosphere when deserts expand, exacerbating global warming.

Afforestation in deserts can reduce the heat transferred to the atmosphere by half. Planting trees for every 10,000km² of desert can reduce atmospheric heat equivalent to 320 million tons of crude oil each year. No other measures can offset global warming at this scale.

Atmospheric heat will be significantly reduced through desertification control, transforming deserts into oases and achieving over 60% forest cover. This fundamentally addresses the issue of excess atmospheric heat and ensures that the amount of heat transfer to the atmosphere is always below the balance point. Consequently, Earth will continue to be an ecological environment and humans will survive.

(3) Mid-Latitude Deserts and Mid-Latitude Westerly Airflows

Mid-latitude regions have favorable temperatures, abundant rainfall, diverse species, and plentiful produce, and should theoretically be located in strategic areas. In reality, most of the world's deserts are located in mid-latitude regions. The Sahara Desert, Arabian Desert, Central Asian Desert, Thar Desert, Taklamakan Desert,

Gobi Desert, and North American Desert are all located in the mid-latitude region, occupying half of the mid-latitude region and damaging the ecological environment. The mid-latitude region is also dominated by westerly airflows. This interaction between mid-latitude westerly airflows and mid-latitude deserts has led to the gradual expansion of deserts, forming a desert belt and arid areas along the mid-latitude zone. Moreover, deserts expand by $60,000km^2$ each year, increasing desertification in the mid-latitude region.

The evaporation of a large amount of water vapor absorbs heat in the Atlantic Ocean, resulting in low temperatures on the ocean surface and at high altitudes. In contrast, the Sahara and Arabian Desert lack ecosystems to absorb solar heat, thus heating the ground and generating a large amount of hot air that rises to high altitudes to form a large area of high temperatures. Air flows from low to high temperature areas. The westerly airflows start to move when the low-temperature water vapor at high altitudes in the Atlantic Ocean flows towards the high-temperature zone of the Sahara and Arabian deserts. The westerly airflows strengthens while passing through the Central Asian Desert, Thar Desert, Taklamakan Desert, and Gobi Desert along the way, as each desert is a high-temperature area at high altitudes and serves as a transmission point for westerly airflows.

Conversely, the strengthened westerly airflows generate a negative suction pressure at a specific speed, taking in the atmosphere's water vapor. Water vapor has a low density and moves upward, making it easier to be sucked into the westerly airflows. Objective and subjective factors contribute to water vapor entering the westerly airflows. This water vapor evaporates from the soil, causing the already dry soil to lose more moisture over time. Under the sun, the dehydrated soil and its overlying air have a higher temperature than soil with plenty of moisture and its overlying air. Low-temperature air flows toward high-temperature air to form wind and sand. The dust particles are carried by wind and sand in larger quantities and over wider areas due to their low density and fine particles. The sand particles are larger with higher density, and mostly remain on the ground after being swept away by the wind. The frequent and repeated "wind and sand sorting" results in a gradual increase in sand particles in the soil, while the proportion of dust particles gradually decreases, leading to desertification. This interaction between mid-latitude deserts and westerly air flows has led to the expansion of deserts by $60,000km^2$ each year, further accelerating desertification in mid-latitude areas. Moreover, "wind and sand sorting" occurs repeatedly as a result of land degradation, and a significant portion of the dust particles in the soil are deposited in the ocean, while sand particles are still deposited on land. This subsequently causes desertification or permafrost, making it difficult for humans to survive.

High-altitude westerly airflows are beyond human control. However, deserts that coexist with these airflows can be managed and regulating westerly airflows is possible through desertification control. First, afforestation in a desert lowers the ground temperature in that area, reduces half of the heat radiated to the atmosphere, and prevents hot air from rising. This will reduce a transmission point for the westerly airflows to strengthen and cause havoc. Transforming multiple deserts into oases will reduce multiple transmission points, weakening the westerly airflows and its interaction with deserts. Westerly airflows will naturally cease to exist when desertification control is a success.

Westerly airflows with a large amount of water vapor pass through high-temperature deserts at high altitudes along the way. This causes a lack of suitable low-temperature environments at high altitudes for precipitation, forming arid zones with little rainfall until they reach the low-temperature area over the ocean surface, where water vapor can condense and precipitate.

Desertification control weakens the westerly airflows, carrying water vapor from the Atlantic and Indian Oceans, and eliminating high-altitude hot environments along the way. This allows the water vapor in the westerly airflows to condense and increase rainfall, transforming the mid-latitude region's arid areas in yellow into a green corridor on Earth, and forming large Amazon forest "lungs" to improve the ecological environment and curb global warming.

There are many forests and a low-temperature environment at high altitudes in west Xinjiang's Yili, resulting in an annual average rainfall of 800mm that is five times more than the annual average rainfall of 147mm in Xinjiang. This suggests that planting trees, increasing forest cover, and lower ground temperatures in arid areas with westerly airflows can promote condensation and precipitation, increase rainfall, and improve ecological conditions.

Desertification control in the mid-latitude region is similar to sailing against the current, where one will fall behind if they do not advance. Without desertification control, deserts will expand by 60,000km^2 every year under the impact of westerly airflows. This is the root cause of the growing intensity of global warming. Humanity will only have a future if desertification control measures are taken.

Ocean surfaces make up most of the ground in low-latitude regions, while a small area of land has vegetation cover and there is no large amount of rising hot air to form westerly airflows. In addition, no hot air rises to form westerly airflows in high-latitude areas because solar radiation is weak, ground temperatures are low, and there are many permafrost zones.

The trajectory of mid-latitude westerly airflows changes from a straight line to a slight arc towards the two polar regions due to the gravitational force of the polar regions.

The interaction between mid-latitude deserts and westerly airflows are currently in the developing and ascending stage as desertification control has not been implemented yet. This will worsen ecological conditions and accelerate global warming. It is not only the root cause of global warming, but will also destroy ecological Earth and humanity. We can only resolve this issue by taking urgent action in reducing desertification.

The interaction between mid-latitude deserts and westerly airflows can explain the role and impact of hot air generated in deserts at high altitudes, causes and effects of the formation of westerly airflows and arid zones in deserts across the world, as well as their interrelationship. These explanations are consistent with the basic theories of natural science and the current situation.

This theory emphasizes the interaction between human and natural conditions and the active role that humans can play in them. It argues that humans can change natural conditions by utilizing the power of nature, rejecting the notion that natural conditions cannot be changed. This theory strengthens humanity's confidence and determination to curb global warming.

This theory further explains the inevitable trend of accelerated global warming as the root cause of the ecological environment and humanity's destruction. It also emphasizes the importance and urgency of global desertification control.

Studies on the interaction between deserts and westerly airflows are just emerging. More research is needed to understand its phenomenon, given that it is a contributing factor to global warming.

(4) Solar Energy is a Double-edged Sword

Solar energy is the most abundant energy source on Earth. It is the source of energy for the growth of living organisms in areas with a good ecological environment, providing conditions beneficial for human survival. However, solar heat is not absorbed and utilized by ecosystems in deserts and arid regions. Instead, it radiates most of the heat to the ground before transferring to the atmosphere, resulting in global warming. Furthermore, it heats the ground and air, raising temperatures, reducing density and rising to high altitudes to form a thermal environment that disrupts the condensation and precipitation of water vapor, and worsens ecological conditions.

The sun raises the temperature when it radiates on the ground and lowers the temperature when it does not shine on the ground, forming significant temperature variations between day and night, and across different terrains and areas. Temperature variations are the driving force behind wind formation, which in turn causes extreme weather and natural disasters. This is a time when solar energy becomes the devil. The role of solar energy as an angel or devil of global warming depends on whether there is an ecosystem that can absorb solar heat. The natural conditions in deserts do not allow the creation of ecosystems that can absorb and utilize solar energy. It can only create droughts and sandstorms, transforming positive energy into negative energy. However, diverting freshwater and creating an ecosystem that can generate water vapor and harness solar energy will convert negative energy into positive energy for the benefit of humanity.

Water, land, and solar energy are the three basic resources on Earth. Water is a cohesive force and core resource. Without water, land will remain a barren wasteland and solar energy can only create droughts and sandstorms.

Water is ordinary, but also magical. In areas where there are no ecosystems, water can absorb the negative solar energy that creates droughts and sandstorms, converting water into water vapor and negative energy to positive energy. The negative solar energy that creates droughts and sandstorms is transformed into the positive energy required for water vapor evaporation. Negative energy is converted to positive energy, water turns into water vapor and becomes the raw material for rain droplets. Water, barren land and solar energy are then integrated as resources and energy for improving ecological conditions.

The amount of solar energy radiating to the Earth each year is essentially constant with little change, but the heat has different effects. Such a huge difference is not because of solar heat itself, but depends on how humans act towards it. If humans are indifferent to it, then deserts and westerly airflows will use global warming as a means and solar energy heat as a butcher knife to destroy the ecological environment and make humans go extinct. Humans must take proactive action in planting trees and implementing desertification control, introduce solar heat into the ecosystem, promote the growth of forests in deserts, build livable environments and combat global warming to ensure human survival. Thus, it is up to humans to determine their fate.

Global warming ultimately boils down to an imbalance in the distribution of solar energy radiating to the Earth, and its heat distribution between the Earth's surface and atmosphere. In short, the excess heat in the atmosphere causes global warming. Forests in deserts can reduce the heat transferred to the atmosphere by half, which is an effective means of regulating the heat distribution ratio. Hence, reducing desertification is necessary in managing the heat distribution ratio on Earth.

(5) High-Altitude Thermal Environment

Will it rain when there is abundant water vapor at high altitudes?

Under normal circumstances, the temperature decreases when altitude increases. Water vapor will rise from an unsaturated state at a higher temperature on the ground to a saturated state at a lower temperature at high altitudes for condensation. The air will also cool at high altitudes, creating a low-temperature environment around the water vapor to condense and form rain droplets. However, there are also exceptions, such as Western Sahara that borders the Atlantic Ocean. Rainfall is still scarce despite no shortage of water vapor at high altitudes, similar to 50mm of rainfall in south Xinjiang, which is far from the ocean.

There is no ecosystem to absorb heat as the sun's rays shine on the desert surface. It can only heat the ground, raise the ground and air temperatures, as well as generate a large amount of hot air, which has a low density and rises to high altitudes. This creates a thermal environment around the water vapor at high altitudes, making it difficult for the water vapor to condense into water droplets. Some condensed water droplets re-evaporate as water vapor, thus it cannot rain even with abundant water vapor. This means that a low-temperature environment around the water vapor at high attitudes is needed for rainfall, apart from abundant water vapor at high altitudes. Condensation is an exothermic reaction where the surrounding low-temperature environment must be able to absorb the released heat for the rain formation process to continue. Therefore, large-scale afforestation must be carried out at deserts to create an ecosystem that can generate water vapor to absorb a large amount of heat, thereby reducing ground temperatures and preventing hot air from rising to form a high-altitude thermal environment that disrupts condensation for rainfall.

Desert and countries near coastal areas can use freshwater resources to implement large-scale afforestation and establish new ecosystems to lower ground temperatures, eliminate high-altitude thermal environments, and allow water vapor to condense and precipitate. New ecosystems also produce a large amount of water vapor ideal for condensation and increased rainfall. As long as there is an area that is large enough with a specific forest cover, high rainfall can be achieved to promote the growth of forests in deserts.

With the interaction between mid-latitude deserts and westerly airflows, deserts are expanding and the heat transferred from deserts to the atmosphere is increasing. This further extends high-altitude thermal environments to other areas. This is a dangerous sign as it will cause a large high-altitude thermal environment over the entire landmass, similar to deserts. It will be difficult to rain even if there is sufficient water vapor. Precipitation on land will significantly decrease and shift to ocean regions with low temperatures. Food cannot be grown on land, and humans will face extinction. The expansion of high-altitude thermal environments is an inevitable consequence of global warming that will destroy humanity.

(6) Climate Change and Global Ecological Environment

Climate change occurs in the atmosphere, but humans cannot regulate the atmosphere. So how can humans tackle climate change?

Climate change and the ecological environment of Earth's land surface are different aspects of human habitats, but they influence each other. The ecological environment of Earth's land surface has a relatively fixed position. On the other hand, the atmosphere at high altitudes does not have a relatively fixed position. The atmosphere and surface are integrated and subject to the Earth's gravitational force. This means that there is a strong relationship between climate change and the ecological environment. There are abundant water vapor and lower temperatures at oceans. In contrast, there is a lack of water vapor and higher temperatures at deserts. The ecological environment of Earth's land surface determine meteorological conditions to an extent, such as temperature, pressure and humidity. Changes in meteorological conditions contribute to climate change. While climate change in the upper atmosphere is beyond human control, we can change the ecological environment of land surfaces. We must start with changing the ecological environment of land surfaces as this is the most direct, effective, and simple approach to addressing climate change.

Climate change is the norm and happening everywhere on Earth. We hope that climate change stays within the normal range of meteorological conditions required for human survival. Extreme weather and natural disasters will occur beyond this normal range, posing a threat to human survival.

However, global warming is not normal. It is a sign that climate change is moving in the wrong direction and threatens human survival, with an increase in the total heat content in the atmosphere, rising temperatures, and elevating temperature variations. Extreme weather and natural disasters will become more frequent and intensify. Thus, humans improve the ecological environment of

Earth's land surface to tackle global warming.

Without understanding the relationship between global warming and the ecological environment, global warming will become "invisible and untouchable". We will not know how to respond, making us helpless and powerless. We can only focus on carbon emissions and use the carbon balance theory to explain global warming, which results in limited understanding and misconceptions. It creates a situation where we can only hope for energy conservation and emissions reduction to succeed in the fight against global warming.

Recognizing the relationship between climate change and the ecological environment of Earth's land surface allows us to understand the direction, path, and measures to curb and reverse global warming. In terms of direction, we should make every effort to reduce the excess heat transfer from the desert surface to the atmosphere. Improving the ecological environment of the Earth's land surface is the path to addressing global warming. Moreover, measures to combat global warming include desertification control, improving global forest cover, and reducing energy consumption and emissions.

Ensuring heat balance will lead us in the right direction, and understanding the relationship between climate change and the ecological environment is the way forward to take effective measures.

(7) Generating Water Vapor is a Powerful Tool for Curbing Global Warming

Most of the water vapor on land comes from oceans. During the hot season, the monsoon circulation of oceans carry a large amount of water vapor flows inland, bringing rainfall and maintaining the water-water vapor-precipitation balance between the Earth's land and oceans.

Land surfaces can evaporate water vapor. They have a strong ability to absorb and store water because trees in forests have strong root systems. Their evaporation of water vapor and intensity of water vapor circulation are greater than in other areas. Forests can also generate water vapor, thus afforestation is an effective means in producing water vapor for increased rainfall.

Ecosystems can absorb and utilize a large amount of solar heat, reducing the amount of heat transferred from the ground to the atmosphere. Most of the existing ecosystems on land were established under the influence of monsoon precipitation on oceans. There are currently two types of areas on land that lack or have insufficient ecosystems – deserts and areas far from oceans, such as northwest China. These areas have the highest heat transfer from the surface to the atmosphere. Developing new ecosystems that can generate water vapor in these areas will play a significant role in improving the ecological environment and tackling global warming.

Humans can create new ecosystems with water vapor

without the limitations of natural rainfall. This can improve ecological conditions, reduce the amount of heat transferred from the ground to the atmosphere, curb global warming, reduce temperature variations, and address climate change. Afforestation is a powerful tool for humanity to combat global warming. Water vapor generated from forests and water vapor transported over oceans can increase rainfall, improve ecological conditions, and reduce temperature variations to tackle climate change, despite evaporation process differences in the two areas. Jiangxi province's Yichun, is used as an example to describe this difference. The forest cover is 63% and 60% in Jiangxi and Yichun, respectively.

1. Different Circulation Routes, Cycles and Frequencies

There is a long monsoon circulation route of water vapor transported over oceans. Water vapor first evaporates from the ocean surface, with the monsoon wind blowing water vapor into inland areas for condensation and precipitation. Rainwater is collected to form streams and rivers before flowing into the sea for evaporation. The entire circulation route takes about 1,200km to Yichun. Although the amount of water vapor circulation is large, the circulation route is long, with a limited annual circulation frequency.

Water vapor generated from forests circulates in situ, where water vapor evaporates from forests and condenses into rain, or dew and frost before entering the soil and evaporation takes place. This water vapor circulation route is short, and takes less time. It has a large number of water vapor circulations in a year, thus inland Yichun has more rainfall than the coastal areas of Hangzhou. The higher number of water vapor circulations plays a significant role in rain formation and ecological improvement.

Climate of Yichun (1971-2000)

Month	Average precipitation (mm)	Number of days with precipitation
January	83	15.5
February	107	15.4
March	177.8	19.5
April	215.9	19.6
May	228.5	18.3
June	243.4	16.2
July	149.5	13.4
August	139.6	13.4
September	81.6	10.3
October	86	11.7
November	69.6	10.3
December	48	9.6
Total	1629.9	174.3

Source: Public Meteorological Service Center of China Meteorological Administration

The data shows the following results:

1) Precipitation from January to June

Yichun recorded 1055.5mm of rainfall in the first half of the year, accounting for 64.75% of the annual precipitation. There were 104.5 days with rainfall, making up 60% of the total number of days with precipitation in a year. During the first half of the year, the ocean surface and land surface temperatures were not high, with a small temperature variation between the ocean and land surfaces. Without the conditions for the formation of rain from the transport of water vapor from oceans, water vapor can only be generated in forests. Yichun received 1,000mm of rainfall in the first half of the year, suggesting that rain formed from the generation of water vapor in forests is comparable to water vapor transported over oceans.

2) Different Precipitation Times

Temperature affects water vapor evaporation. The saturated vapor pressure at 36 degrees Celsius is 2.25 times that at 22 degrees Celsius. During the hot season of July, August and September, there was a large amount of water vapor evaporation from the ocean surface, enabling the monsoon wind to blow a large amount of water vapor into inland areas. Due to the long circulation route, a huge amount of energy is needed to drive the monsoon wind. This requires a large temperature variation as the driving force. A large temperature variation between the inland areas and oceans can only be seen during the hot season, promoting the formation of strong monsoon winds over oceans. Therefore, rainfall mostly occurs during the hot season of July, August and September. Water vapor diffusion over short distances is only possible during other months.

Forest-generated water vapor is different, where an insufficient amount of water vapor is maintained throughout the year. Yichun has more than 10 days of rainfall each month, with some dry months.

3) Different Rainfall Patterns

Oceanic monsoon climate not only brings a large amount of water vapor but is also driven by strong winds caused by large temperature variations. Multiple typhoons will occur during the hot season of July, August and September, bringing heavy rain that cause flooding, mudslides and landslides in river basins, threatening people's lives and property.

There are many trees, and small temperature variations between different areas in Yichun. Wind speeds generally do not exceed Level 3-4 in the city. Yichun has the highest rainfall in June with 243.4mm and 16.2 days of precipitation, averaging 15mm a day. This indicates that the city mostly experiences light showers or moderate rain, and heavy rain on some days. Moderate and light rain is easily absorbed and stored by the soil, which is beneficial for agriculture and forestry.

4) Different Degrees of Controllability

Water vapor transported over oceans is determined by natural conditions and beyond human control. On the other hand, water vapor generated from forests can be controlled and regulated to an extent. Large-scale afforestation, production of water vapor from forests, and increased local rainfall will improve the ecological environment. This demonstrates that humans have some control in combating global warming.

A sizeable forest cover is needed as a large forest acts like a big reservoir. There is significant water and water vapor circulation, but a small amount of water and water vapor that diffuses out of the forest periphery into the surrounding area. The entire forest can maintain a balance between soil water storage, evaporation and precipitation. The ecosystem can still survive and develop, even without external water resources. The 63% forest cover in Jiangxi province ensures good environmental conditions for generating water vapor in Yichun.

The amount of water and water vapor circulation will not be large without a sizeable forest. The amount of water and water vapor that diffuses out of the forest periphery into the surrounding area accounts for a significant proportion of the total amount. The amount of water and water vapor circulation in the forest will decrease, limiting the role of forests in increasing rainfall.

The inland areas of Jiangxi province receives less water vapor transported over oceans than coastal provinces, but it has the second highest forest cover of 63% in China — exceeding that of coastal provinces such as Zhejiang, Guangdong, Guangxi and Jiangsu. This indicates the significant role of rainfall through water vapor generated from forests in increasing forest cover.

Everything has two sides. Abundant rainfall comes with a high level of humidity, thus food and other items are prone to mold. Humidity control and mold prevention are essential aspects of daily life.

Yichun has a mixed rainfall pattern of water vapor generated from forests and ocean water vapor. From January to June, evaporation of water vapor generated from forests increased, water vapor circulation accelerated, and rainfall grew month by month as temperatures rise. Strong ocean monsoons arrive in July, August and September, forming a mixed precipitation pattern of water vapor generated from forests and ocean water vapor. However, Yichun is 600km away from the East China Sea where ocean water vapor condenses and precipitates along the way. Thus, the water vapor content has already decreased when it reaches Yichun despite the strong currents. A total of 149.5mm of rainfall was recorded in July, a decrease of 93.9mm from June. The arrival of monsoon over oceans reduced precipitation, indicating that rainfall from ocean monsoon is not necessarily higher than rainfall formed from water vapor generated in forests. The data further showed that precipitation had been decreasing after July as the ocean monsoon gradually weakens and temperatures continue to drop. This reflects the basic trend and law of alternating mixed precipitation of water vapor generated from forests and water vapor transported over oceans.

Based on Yichun's meteorological data over 30 years, a new cyclical balance relationship of water-water vapor generated from forests-precipitation is predicted to be established in deserts and arid areas worldwide after utilizing freshwater, adopting afforestation and establishing new ecosystems with water vapor produced from forests. This can be described as a new "artificial and natural rainfall linkage" desert model, where total rainfall will increase, and monthly precipitation will also grow with rising temperatures and decrease with falling temperatures. Rainfall will be more frequent, longer, and in the form of moderate or light rain, which is beneficial for agriculture and forestry.

The larger the forest area and the higher the forest cover, the greater the amount of water vapor generated and circulated, resulting in increased rainfall.

Yichun is not a special case but serves to illustrate the situation.

The climate data in Anhui province's Huangshan also demonstrates this point. The following table shows its climate data from 1971 to 2000.

Climate of Huangshan (1971-2000)

Month	Average precipitation (mm)	Number of days with precipitation	Average daily rainfall (mm)
1	78.7	14	5.61
2	111.3	14.7	7.57
3	182.3	18.4	9.9
4	232.6	17.6	13.2
5	273.3	18	15.18

6	485.5	18.1	25.3
7	335.2	16.3	20.56
8	305.3	18.2	16.77
9	180.1	14.5	12.42
10	111.2	12.1	9.19
11	82.7	9.7	8.5
12	50.5	8.9	5.6
Total	2402.3	180.5	12.48

The data showed that precipitation increased with rising temperatures from January to June, with the highest precipitation recorded in June — similar to Yichun.

The highly daily rainfall was 25.3mm with moderate or light rain. This situation is also similar to Yichun.

There were more than nine days of rainfall each month, with some dry days, similar to Yichun.

In addition, Huangshan's high forest cover and precipitation exceeding 1,000mm in the first half of the year were similar to Yichun.

These similarities indicate that areas with high forest cover have comparable climate change patterns.

It is also a common pattern to see high forest cover resulting in more rainfall.

Comparison between Anhui province and Huangshan

Location	Forest cover (%)	Annual rainfall (mm)
Anhui Province	28.65	1200
Huangshan, Anhui	82.9	2402

The data further demonstrates that more trees will boost rainfall, and water vapor generated from forests is an essential source for increasing precipitation. More rain also facilitates the growth of more trees, forming a beneficial cycle in the ecosystem. Hence, afforestation is an effective measure to increase local precipitation.

Water vapor transported over oceans and forest-generated water vapor can both become raw materials for rainfall. Compared to the two, water vapor generated from forests has more advantages in terms of the number of water cycles, the rainfall time span, precipitation patterns, as well as stability and uniformity of precipitation.

Throughout history, all human activities cannot escape the control of nature. Low precipitation and poor ecological conditions are naturally formed in deserts and arid regions, leaving people with no choice but let nature take its course. Water vapor generated from forests made people realize that it is possible to use external water resources, harness solar energy and utilize land to develop forests, increase precipitation, create new ecological conditions, re-create a beautiful ecological environment, and ensure a harmonious co-existence between humans and nature.

The success of this concept depends on whether rainfall can meet the growth needs of the newly built forests in the long term. Rainfall in newly built forests consists of two parts — rainfall from the condensation of existing water vapor in the upper atmosphere after the high-altitude thermal environment disappears. The other is rainfall from the condensation of water vapor generated from newly built forests. Whether the sum of these two parts of rainfall can meet the growth needs of the forest is the prerequisite for the survival and development of forests. The production of water vapor at high altitudes also depends on the existence of forests. Lowering ground temperatures, preventing the generation of hot air, and preventing the formation of a high-altitude thermal environment are all prerequisites to produce water vapor in forests. Ultimately, the survival of newly built forests depend on their ability to generate water vapor for precipitation. Therefore, water vapor produced by forests is crucial for determining whether deserts and arid regions can be afforested and survive in the long term.

The belief that "rain depends on nature, not humans" is a long-standing perception. The idea of water vapor generated from forests aims to establish a new perspective that rain depends on both nature and human effort. By creating a new "artificial and natural linkage" model, we can utilize water resources and land, as well as harness solar energy to promote afforestation in deserts. By generating water vapor in forests, we can explore new methods to increase rainfall and develop the interaction between nature and humans.

Diverting water from Tibet to Xinjiang to increase rainfall in Xinjiang and northwest China represents a new "artificial and natural rainfall linkage" model.

(8) Spreading Effect of Ecosystem

A large amount of water vapor can be generated to increase precipitation when afforestation is carried out in deserts and man-made forests create new ecosystems. Forests in deserts lower ground temperatures and eliminate high-altitude thermal environments, allowing existing water vapor in the upper atmosphere to condense and precipitate. Both factors contribute to increased rainfall. The amount of diverted water can be gradually reduced when precipitation increases to a level that can meet the growth needs of artificial forests. The surplus water can be diverted to other deserts to develop new forests. This allows water resources to be utilized multiple times and in various locations. Afforestation can proceed, and new ecosystems can continue to be created and expanded. This process can be called the "spreading effect of ecosystems", making it feasible to implement desertification control. However, it is impossible to solve water issues for afforestation in deserts all at once, given the vast size of deserts worldwide. It is also impossible for forests in deserts to rely on external water supply for growth and survival in the long term. With the "spreading effect of ecosystems", global desertification control can be carried out in phases. Forests in deserts can rely on its water vapor and elimination of high-altitude thermal environments, as well as condensation of existing water vapor in the upper atmosphere for increased rainfall, facilitating its growth. Water for afforestation can also be supplied in phases and batches, allowing tree-planting to continue. Global desertification control can be completed within 100 years or longer. The "spreading effect of ecosystems" turns global desertification control from impossible to possible.

There is a causal relationship between developing water vapor from forests and the "spreading effect of ecosystems". Generating water vapor from forests is needed for the "spreading effect of ecosystems" to make an impact.

Human will is needed to develop water vapor from forests, utilizing the power of nature to improve the relationship between humans and nature and make global desertification control possible. Developing water vapor and promoting the "spreading effect of ecosystems" can realize global desertification control. This means that it is time for humans to take control of their destiny, marking a turning point in human history.

The "spreading effect of ecosystems" ensures sustainability and makes global desertification control feasible.

(9) Comparison of Two Theories

Studies on global warming focus on the greenhouse effect. The atmospheric heat theory based on heat transfer in deserts is now proposed as the key to understanding global warming. The two theories have different ideas, directions, paths, and measures. We should use the theory that is more consistent with reality and can guide future measures. The section below is a comparison of the two theories from various aspects.

1. Foresight

The atmospheric heat theory examines the causes of global warming from both natural and anthropogenic factors, distinguishing between the main and secondary causes, focusing on managing the main causes, and addressing the secondary causes to control various heat transfer channels that affect global warming.

The greenhouse effect only takes into account man-made carbon emissions, believing it to be the main cause of global warming while overlooking the natural factors.

The lack of foresight leads to treating secondary causes as main causes in addressing global warming.

2. Chain of Action

The atmospheric heat theory focuses on atmospheric heat as the central issue, linking various elements to form a complete chain of action.

The atmospheric heat theory's chain of action is comprehensive, which includes desertification control as the main chain and improving forest cover and reducing

121

energy consumption and emissions as the chain's branches. These chains can clearly explain the roles of each process, their interrelationships, and maintain the heat balance relationship of each process.

Desertification control is the main chain of action. The heat transferred to the atmosphere through deserts alone can exceed the atmospheric heat redline and complete the entire action chain process independently.

Improving global forest cover is a branch chain of action. The heat transmitted to the atmosphere can maintain a normal heat balance between the Earth's surface and atmosphere. There is not enough heat to break through the atmospheric heat redline.

The heat of fuel combustion transferred to the atmosphere is also a branch chain of action. The amount of heat transmitted to the atmosphere is only 0.2% of the heat transferred from the desert surface in a year. This makes it impossible to break through the atmospheric heat redline independently.

The main chain of action can act independently throughout the entire process. The branch chains can only be inserted into the first part of the main chain and cannot independently form a new chain of action. Branch action chains cannot balance heat on their own.

3. Relationship and Difference between Global Warming and Greenhouse Effect

Global warming is a natural phenomenon caused by

the combined effects of natural and anthropogenic factors. Natural causes are multifaceted, including heat transfer from the desert surface to the atmosphere. This is a one-directional increase that is irreversible, accelerating global warming and posing a serious threat to human survival.

Anthropogenic factors involve the burning of fossil fuels. The greenhouse effect should refer to the heat effect caused by the partial heat from burning of carbon fuel and absorption of carbon dioxide in the atmosphere. However, the amount of heat entering the atmosphere is equivalent to 4 billion tons of crude oil each year, or 0.2% of the annual amount of heat transferred from desert surfaces to the atmosphere. Thus, the greenhouse effect is limited and insignificant in affecting global warming. Greenhouse gases are not the main cause of global warming.

The concept of the greenhouse effect has been changed. The heat from greenhouse effect comes from part of the heat generated from burning of fossil fuels. The term greenhouse effect remains unchanged, but the heat referred here includes heat transferred from the surface to the atmosphere, which is 500 times greater than heat released from fuel combustion. This greenhouse effect is no longer the real greenhouse effect but a false greenhouse effect that has been magnified by over 500 times. This causes confusion on the greenhouse effect and atmospheric heat concepts, and the cause of global warming is attributed to fuel combustion.

The atmosphere is heated by the absorption of heat by various gaseous elements in the atmosphere, including water vapor, carbon dioxide and nitrogen.

Oceans make up two-thirds of the Earth's surface, and evaporates a large amount of water vapor. Land occupies the remaining one-third of the Earth's surface, and also evaporates water vapor. Thus, there is more water vapor content in the atmosphere than carbon dioxide. Moreover, the specific heat capacity of water vapor is also greater than that of carbon dioxide. This means that water vapor can absorb more heat than carbon dioxide in the atmosphere. In terms of heat absorption of gaseous elements, studies usually exaggerate the role of carbon dioxide, while overlooking water vapor. This is done to prove that carbon emissions are the main cause of global warming.

Global warming is a thermal phenomenon caused by the absorption of heat from various sources that are then transferred to the atmosphere. Deserts account for the majority of this heat transfer.

Global warming's heat capacity is hundreds of times greater than that of the greenhouse effect. It is misleading to say that the greenhouse effect is the main cause of global warming. Its greatest danger is that it conceals the biggest and most important cause of global warming. Ultimately, it will lead people to take ineffective countermeasures, and wait for ecological Earth to be destroyed and humans to go extinct.

Carbon emissions have been reduced following global

efforts to reduce energy consumption and emissions over the past few decades. If global warming is caused by excess carbon emissions, global warming should have slowed down by now. However, the reality is global warming is getting worse. The Northern Hemisphere had set new record high temperatures and droughts in 2022 and 2023, clearly showing that it is an illusion to regard reducing energy consumption and emissions as the key to combat global warming. Hence, we must drop this illusion and find another solution.

(10) The Three Strategic Measures Can Curb Global Warming

Curbing global warming is a monumental task that requires generations of tireless efforts to achieve results. The three strategic measures of desertification control, improving forest cover, as well as reducing energy consumption and emissions must work in tandem to tackle global warming. The three measures utilize human intelligence and harness the power of nature to transform the world.

Desertification control is the most arduous and challenging task among the three measures. However, we are confident that desertification control will work for the following reasons:

1. We can utilize trillions of cubic meters of freshwater that flow into the sea each year, 30 million square kilometers of desert land, and solar heat that is hundreds of

times greater than the global annual consumption of carbon energy. The planting of trees can transform forest resources into wealth, serving as a material basis, improving the ecological environment and combating global warming.

2. The "spreading effect of ecosystems" allows afforestation to continue the greening of deserts step by step. These little steps will eventually help achieve the goal of desertification control.

3. There is strong momentum for implementation. Through afforestation and ecological methods, transforming ineffective resources and energy sources on Earth into immense wealth is a big pie for global wealth distribution. Investors and participants will be the beneficiaries of economic interests. Curbing global warming and resolving the survival crisis benefits everyone on Earth, aligning with the interests of all humans.

Saving humanity is a life-and-death battle between survival and extinction. There is only one way forward for humanity: fight with all our might.

Desertification in mid-latitude regions has been ongoing for thousands of years. However, turning deserts into oases only takes a few decades, a process that is much faster than desertification. Hence, we are confident that reducing desertification can be achieved within 100 years or longer, as long as we take action and through generations of unwavering efforts.

Countries with deserts should focus on managing their

deserts, while countries without deserts can increase their forest cover and participate in desertification control efforts. The three strategic measures can mobilize every country, individual, piece of land, and tree on Earth to contribute to tackling global warming, creating a powerful force that has the potential to resolve the human survival crisis. Natural resources and energy are inexhaustible, and the benefits of nature are immense and boundless. Seeking benefits for humanity requires us to understand nature and follow its laws to guide us in the right direction.

www.ingramcontent.com/pod-product-compliance
Lightning Source LLC
Chambersburg PA
CBHW030811280326
41926CB00085B/472